Hand in Hand

Partners Working Together with God

Betty Jo Lewis

Woman's Missionary Union
Birmingham, Alabama

This book is a resource in the Christian Growth Study Plan (formerly Church Study Course). You can receive credit two ways: (1) read the book and attend a 2½-hour study; (2) read the book, write a summary of each chapter, then show your work to a church leader. For a credit request form, and more information about the Christian Growth Study Plan, refer to the current Christian Growth Study Plan Catalog. Someone in your church office may have a copy, or you may receive a free copy by contacting the Christian Growth Study Plan office, 127 Ninth Avenue, North, MSN 117, Nashville, TN 37234-0117, phone (615) 251-2525.

Woman's Missionary Union
P. O. Box 830010
Birmingham, AL 35283-0010
©1996 by Woman's Missionary Union

Dewey Decimal Classification: 248.4
Subject Headings: CHRISTIAN LIFE
                  GOD (CHRISTIANITY)
                  MINISTRY
                  WOMEN—BIBLICAL TEACHING

ISBN: 1-56309-163-1

W963103•0496•15M1

Contents

Preface

The day at my house was rather ordinary. I was routinely doing household chores, returning phone calls, and writing notes and letters. While sorting the mail, I spied the familiar stationery of Woman's Missionary Union in Birmingham. It was a letter from Judith Edwards, design editor. Standing by my kitchen counter, I opened the envelope and began reading her friendly greeting and then, "I am writing to ask you to consider being the writer for our WMU emphasis book for 1996-97."

My knees weakened as strength seeped from my body. I sank into a chair at the kitchen table thinking, "No, no, that's impossible. I can't write a book." My heart raced as if I were in aerobics class. I tried to comprehend the request and the magnitude of such a task.

On the table, my Bible was opened to a passage I had been reading earlier. While my brain began to list reasons I could not accept such an assignment, my eyes fell on these verses: "Such confidence as this is ours through Christ before God. Not that we are competent in ourselves to claim anything for ourselves, but our competence comes from God" (2 Cor. 3:4-5 NIV).

It was as if God were saying to me, "You're right, Betty Jo, you can't write a book. But if you'll take this assignment and acknowledge you can't do it, then I'll do it through you."

"Oh, loving Father, will you partner with me to accomplish such a task? Can my hands be God's hands?"

Betty Jo Lewis
Atlanta, Georgia

Introduction

God is at work in our world today. Barriers of igno-rance, poverty, apathy, culture, and race are coming down as people of God surrender to God. God's hands are on our lives, making a difference in us and in our world.

The Scriptures are replete with teachings about God's hands and our hands. Over and over, we are urged to let God touch our world through us.

People are enduring much suffering and pain. In our world children are suffering, and they have no legislative voice. Women are abused and exploited. People of every race and culture are trying to find their niche. They all need to know Jesus, our best friend, and they need you and me to be a friend to them. They need an advocate, a helping hand, a word of encouragement, and an arm around their shoulder.

We must be pliable clay in the Potter's hands and al-low God to minister in and through us. For God to work through us, we must put our hands in His. Then hand in hand, we can partner to accomplish His work.

"For we are partners working together for God, and you are God's field. You are also God's building" (1 Cor. 3:9 TEV).

CHAPTER ONE

Hand in Hand with God

Who Is God?

"In the beginning, God, not nothing; for if there had been nothing, that's all there ever would have been." That thought, whose author is unknown to me, expresses my absolute belief in the reality and necessity of the supreme and sovereign God as the designer of our world and the origin of all life on our planet. God is preexistent. He has always been. Without Him, life on earth would have never been. "Holy, holy, holy is the Lord God Almighty, who was, and is, and is to come" (Rev. 4:8*b* NIV). People of the earth are the "field and building" of God . . . the tangible fruit of His creativity. We existed first in the heart and mind of God, and now He desires to inhabit us.

The amazing truth I have come to appreciate while writing this book is that holy and sovereign God planned from the beginning to work through His children. The Creator, the Father, the Holy Trinity, the Author and Finisher of our faith wants to partner with us, hand in hand, to accomplish His work in our world.

An examination of who God is reminds me of His sovereignty, His absolute originality. He is autonomous and authentic. Yet, in the light of such authentic holiness, He has made it possible for us to be reconciled to Him through His Son, Jesus Christ, our Savior. Sovereign God conceived the plan of salvation and made it available to us through the blood sacrifice of Jesus Christ. When we by faith receive Jesus, we become children of God (see John 1:1-12).

However, there is great temptation for me to serve God motivated by desire for merit and recognition rather than simply as a vessel in His hands. My self-centered human condition sets me up for such ill-motivated service rather than my acknowledgement of Christ's living in me and wanting to work through me.

Because of this, my life verse is: "I have been crucified with Christ and I no longer live, but Christ lives in me. The life I live in the body, I live by faith in the Son of God, who loved me and gave himself for me" (Gal. 2:20 NIV).

Dissension caused by human selfishness has always been a problem. The church at Corinth experienced division when they judged others by the human standards of prestige and status. Jealous of one another, they quarreled about who was the most important—those baptized by Paul or those baptized by Apollos. They, like us at times, seemed oblivious to the One who was really responsible for their salvation.

"What, after all, is Apollos? And what is Paul? Only servants, through whom you came to believe—as the Lord has assigned to each his task. I planted the seed, Apollos watered it, but God made it grow" (1 Cor. 3:5-6 NIV).

Paul, as a servant of God, pled with the Corinthians to acknowledge their flawed thinking. He wanted them to realize that he had planted the seed of salvation by giving them the gospel; Apollos had watered it by teaching them doctrine; but God had caused the seed to grow in their hearts. So God works hand in hand with His servants to reap the harvest.

God is perfectly capable of doing His work alone, but He has chosen to work through His servants. God allows His servants the joy of cultivation and the joy of partaking in the blessings of harvest.

Departing Words

The last words of a dying loved one are a treasure. And if those last words are a request, the family goes to any length to fulfill it. Before Jesus left His followers to return to the Heavenly Father, He shared some last words. We call them the Great Commission.

"Then Jesus came to them and said, 'All authority in heaven and on earth has been given to me. Therefore go and make disciples of all nations, baptizing them in the name of the Father and of the Son and of the Holy Spirit, and teaching them to obey everything I have commanded you. And surely I am with you always, to the very end of the age' " (Matt. 28:18-20 NIV).

My husband likes to remind me (and everyone else to whom he preaches) that the Great Commission is not the Great Suggestion. It is actually a command and a declaration of truth. And if we are obedient followers, we will obey His command.

God has not left His servants powerless and unequipped. Acts 1:8 promises us the power that Jesus Christ claimed as His own in Matthew 28:18, and verses 19 and 20 give us the plan: disciples are to make disciples of all people. We have the promise of the presence of God with us to the end of the age. And so, we are commissioned ones.

Greater Works

"I tell you the truth, anyone who has faith in me will do what I have been doing. He will do even greater things than these, because I am going to the Father" (John 14:12 NIV).

Jesus actually said this to His disciples before He departed for heaven. It has baffled disciples through the ages. How can we finite beings do greater things than Jesus? Are our works greater in quality or quantity, or both? Jesus was probably implying the breadth of our works as well as the excellence. At the time, Jesus could foresee many future believers ministering for hundreds of years, resulting in His followers doing greater things, especially in quantity, than He. The earthly ministry of Jesus lasted only three years. He, by choice, was limited by time and space while on earth. Then He returned to the Father.

The wonderful truth is that God, for reasons known only to Him, has chosen to work in and through people. I'm sure we would have come up with a plan very different from infinite God's. A people plan would surely have been more grandiose!

Jesus Christ is to be lifted up. In this exalted state, He promises to draw people to Himself. We lift Christ up by honoring Him with our lifestyle and by taking the initiative to share the gospel. Jesus is lifted up by our caring and sensitive ministry to others. God has chosen to allow human beings to be partners with Him in accomplishing His task, His mission on earth.

God does not leave us alone in the task. Our greater works will actually be accomplished by the Counselor, the Holy Spirit, in and through us. "But you will receive power when the Holy Spirit comes on you; and you will be my witnesses in Jerusalem, and in all Judea and Samaria, and to the ends of the earth" (Acts 1:8 NIV).

Earlier, Jesus had tried to comfort His disciples with the promise of the Counselor—the Spirit of truth. "But I tell you the truth: It is for your good that I am going away. Unless I go away, the Counselor will not come to you; but if I go, I will send him to you. I have much more to say to you, more than you can now bear. But when he, the Spirit of truth, comes, he will guide you into all truth. He will not speak on his own; he will speak only what he hears, and he will tell you what is yet to come. He will bring glory to me by taking from what is mine and making it known to you" (John 16:7, 12-15 NIV).

Look at what Jesus did when He was on earth. See Him healing all kinds of diseases and even changing physical death into life. When have we done these things? But then, see Him teaching, showing compassion to all kinds of people, and praying relentlessly for the Father's will to be accomplished. In continuing these things that Jesus did, we are doing greater works. Our hand-in-hand partnership with God is limited only by our disobedience, unfaithfulness, and rebellion.

A hand-in-hand partnership with God demands an unalterable focus on God through prayer and Bible study. Each day must begin with a denial of self and a promise to God to live in obedience for that day. Once we promise to obey God, He will direct us and order our activities of the day.

Many times in our zealous desire to serve—and remembering the promise of greater works—we rush headlong into church work which we assume or hope to be the greater works. We pump our egos with satisfactory results and run on to the next thing that we are "doing for God."

Without Him, We Can Do Nothing

Jesus reminds us in John 5:17 that God is constantly at work in our world. And as John 15:5 says, without Him we can do nothing. And so it behooves us to answer the question anew in our hearts, Who is God? Without Him, nothing of any lasting value is done. "[A]ll our righteous acts are like filthy rags" (Isa. 64:6*b* NIV).

I can do nothing to commend myself to Him. When, in my own eyes, I have been successful in doing a work for Christ, in my power and on a foundation of my own making, my "work will be shown for what it is, because the Day will bring it to light. It will be revealed with fire, and the fire will test the quality of each man's work" (1 Cor. 3:13 NIV). Salvation is and was God's idea. He chose you. He chose me. We may never understand why, yet His love for us is unconditional. As finite humans, we can neither fathom nor quite grasp the lovely reality of God's agape love.

Knowing our human limitations yet desiring to make us partners in His work, God gifted us and equipped us with the Counselor, the Holy Spirit, and allowed us to be part of His mission in our world. There is something all of us can do. Isn't it just like God not to leave out a single one of His children?

We often hear the missions challenge expressed like this: we can all give, go, or pray. When I was in Girls' Auxiliary (now Girls in Action), I learned that proper stewardship is giving time, money, and personality. Some of us are more gifted in the area of time, others in the area of possessions, and still others in personality, possessing qualities of leadership and creativity that God loves to utilize in His work.

Prayer is something we all can do—from the oldest to the youngest. I believe, however, the kind of powerful, effective, righteous praying for missions described in James 5 is a special gift. It is given to one with a heart for God, a heart for missions, and a skill for organizing needs and information. The missions "pray-er" is aware that one special avenue God walks down to do His work is prayer. Our missionaries on the field feel so dependent on the prayers offered in their behalf. They often vow they will come home if the praying stops.

That is not likely to happen as long as there are people like the teenager we met in Oklahoma. She showed us her lunch box full of 3-by-5 inch cards. Missionary names and prayer requests were recorded on the cards. She explained that every night before bed, she called the Home and Foreign Mission Boards' PrayerLines to hear the current prayer needs. After writing on the cards, she put them in her lunch box to take to school the next day. Then, at every opportunity she lifted the missionary and the request to God in prayer.

In *Shadowlands,* a movie about C.S. Lewis, Lewis said this after the untimely death of his beloved wife, Joy: "I pray because I can't help myself. Prayer doesn't change God, it changes me." A commitment to the second part of that missions expression . . . going . . . often occurs during or as a result of the acts of praying and giving, and as a direct result of missions awareness, as we receive information and reports from the missions fields.

We are partners with working together with God. Our hands can be God's hands.

CHAPTER TWO

Our Hands, God's Hands

In Scripture, references to hands are both literal and poetic. Hands symbolize power and position as well as action. To the artist, the hand embodies grace, strength, and beauty.

In daily living, the hand enables us to complete ordinary tasks. People who have lost their hands, or the use of them, must train other body parts or use artificial instruments to perform the tasks that were once performed with their hands.

Hands touch, hold, and grasp objects. The grasping procedure is proficient because of our unique opposing thumbs. Try picking up a pen or pencil without your thumb—not impossible, but awkward. The fingers on our hands are capable of operating independently as when playing the piano, or together, as when clutching a ball and bat.

Look at your hands. Make a fist. Point a finger. Clap. Hands truly are an amazing part of the human anatomy. The hand is made of slender bones, tendons, and muscle tissue. The Creator gave grace and mobility to our hands by backing them up with muscles in the forearms. Therefore, fingers are mobile and can perform delicate tasks without bulky muscle tissue interfering.

Our hands deliver the sense of touch to our brains. We feel pressure, temperature, and pain with our hands. Frequently blind people develop a sensitivity that enables them to "read" with their hands.

The Touch of Human Hands
The touch of human hands—
That is the boon we ask;
For groping, day by day,
Along the stony way,
We need the comrade heart
That understands,
And the warmth, the living warmth
Of human hands.

The touch of human hands;
Not vain, unthinking words,
Nor that cold charity
Which shuns our misery;
We seek a loyal friend
Who understands,
And the warmth, the pulsing warmth
Of human hands.

The touch of human hands—
Such care as was in him
Who walked in Galilee
Beside the silver sea;
We need a patient guide
Who understands,
And the warmth, the loving warmth
Of human hands.[1]

Thomas Curtis Clark

With a touch, a squeeze, a hug, hands give comfort. Hands squeezed into a fist can hurt or scare. Hands joined with other hands bind covenants. Hands are raised in promises, oaths, or demonstrations of power and authority. Hands affirm with applause and wave in expressions of friendship. Hands demean others with slaps of anger. Hands keep rhythm to a musical beat.

Some of us who speak with our mouths are accused of "talking" with our hands, while others communicate with sign language. Some use the hand in combination with a writing instrument to communicate through notes, letters, articles, or books. The right hand is said to denote power; in some cultures, the left hand of a woman becomes prominent when it bears an engagement ring. We should thank God for these wonderful tools, our hands, and dedicate them to His service so they become instruments of blessing and not cursing.

Hands in Scripture

Throughout the Bible hands are used to communicate literal and symbolic meanings. Here are a few examples:

Elisha is described as a prophet in 2 Kings 3:11 because he "poured water on the hands of Elijah."

Pilate declared his innocence of a man's blood with the Old Testament practice of washing his hands (Deut. 21:6-8) before the crowd (Matt. 27:24).

A kiss on the hand implies enticement and homage in Job 31:27.

The hand is raised in taking an oath in Genesis 14:22.

Aaron lifted his hands to bless the people in Leviticus 9:22.

A hand lifted against David is an act of rebellion in 2 Samuel 20:21.

The offer of a hand signifies one accord in 2 Kings 10:15.

The Lord at one's right hand denotes protection and support in Psalms 16:8 and 109:31.

"At hand" is a figure of speech indicating immediacy of the event in Matthew 26:18 (KJV).

The laying on of hands signifies blessing and mission in the lives of Barnabas and Saul, the first deacons (Acts 6:6; 13:3).

Hands convey power, friendship, blessing, and curses. "Whatever your hand finds to do, do it with all your might" (Eccl. 9:10*a*).

God's Hands

God doesn't have physical hands. He doesn't need hands. God speaks and it happens. However, the hand or hands of God are mentioned throughout Scripture to help our finite minds visualize His working. We are better able to relate to God's working when His deeds are described as being done with His hands.

God *spoke* the world into being. But more seemed to be involved with the creation of man and woman. He *formed* Adam and Eve, implying a more personal use of hands and signifying the intimate relationship and fellowship we enjoy with our Creator/Father.

First Samuel 5:6 says the Lord's hand is heavy, denoting strength, oppression, and control.

The hand of God is a place of protection, provision, and position for us. Jesus declared to the Jews that He and the Father are one. To the believers who are described as sheep, Jesus is the shepherd, protecting and providing for His sheep forever. Jesus called the hand of the Father the safest, most secure place. It is impossible for sheep to be snatched from His hand (see John 10:28-30).

The late Bertha Smith, missionary to China, taught that John 14:20 describes the secure position of Christians. Using a simple and personal illustration, she would say, "There are only two sides of me, the inside and the outside." She would draw a big circle on the chalkboard which represented God, then draw a smaller circle inside to represent Jesus, Whom the Scriptures say is inside the Father. She drew another circle inside the Jesus circle, representing herself in Jesus. Then she drew a small circle inside her circle to represent Jesus inside her.

Miss Smith declared, "And verse 20 promises Jesus is in the Father. As a believer, I am in Jesus and Jesus is in me. And that covers both sides of me, the inside and outside." She had been a missionary during the Japanese invasion of China, and even in such danger, was convinced of her security in the Father's hands.

We are safe in the Father's hands. Nothing reaches us without passing through the permissive will of Jesus and the Father. What a marvelous place of protection and provision for believers—in the hands of the Father.

The psalmist declared his faith in God's protection: "Your hand will guide me, your right hand will hold me fast" (Psalm 139:10). All Christians everywhere are told to "humble yourselves, therefore, under God's mighty hand, that he may lift you up in due time" (1 Peter 5:6).

Jesus, at His atoning death on the cross, declared His work of salvation to be finished and cried aloud, "Father, into your hands I commit my spirit" (Luke 23:46).

Though Daniel warned Belshazzar of the mighty hand of God, Belshazzar did not honor God, even though God held Belshazzar's life in His hands. So God sent a hand to write a message of doom on the wall for Belshazzar (Dan. 5:23-24). We are told that "it is a dreadful thing to fall into the hands of the living God" (Heb. 10:31).

The Hands of Jesus

Jesus' hands were prominent during His earthly ministry in both a literal and poetic sense. As an apprentice carpenter, His hands were tools for the trade that provided material resources for His family. Skillfully and tenaciously, He must have used His hands to turn rough cedar logs into smooth furniture or fashion stone into building blocks.

As He began His journey to Calvary, the people heard Him teach in the synagogue and said with wonderment, "What wisdom is this which is given unto him, that even such mighty works are wrought by his hands?" (Mark 6:2*b* KJV).

Jesus had purpose and a vision; He knew where He came from and where He was going. Jesus knew God had "given all things into his hands" (John 13:3 KJV). With this awareness, Jesus personified humility, pouring water into a basin and then washing and drying the disciples' feet. Simon Peter balked, declaring his feet would never be washed by Jesus' hands. Jesus tenderly explained the meaning behind the deed. Peter could not always do for Jesus. Peter had to receive from Jesus as well. Then Peter exclaimed, "[Then wash] not just my feet but my hands and my head as well!" (John 13:9). Jesus used His hands to teach the disciples and us to serve one another.

The hands of Jesus brought judgment. Once the Pharisees piously brought a woman caught in adultery to Jesus, demanding that He pronounce the judgment of Moses' Law on her. With His hand, Jesus wrote something in the dust that convicted and scared the men as they felt the judgment of Jesus on themselves. Each one left the scene. Jesus was alone with the accused woman. He tenderly sent her on her way, admonishing her to "leave [her] life of sin" (John 8:11*b*).

Jesus' hands often brought blessing. With His hands He blessed children and babies. His hands broke bread and fed thousands. His hands made a blind man see.

Thomas, the one we call the Doubter, wanted to believe that Jesus had been resurrected from the dead. But it just seemed too good to be true. Thomas demanded to see the hands of Jesus, to feel the marks left by the nails, and to put his own hands into the wound in Jesus' side. Jesus allowed Thomas that privilege, saying, " 'Put your finger here; see my hands. Reach out your hand and put it into my side. Stop doubting and believe.' Thomas said to him, 'My Lord and my God!' Then Jesus told him, 'Because you have seen me, you have believed; blessed are those who have not seen and yet have believed' " (John 20:24-31). Neither you nor I have seen with our eyes or felt with our hands. Have we cried, "My Lord and my God!"? Do we believe? Are we available?

No human has ever suffered, or will ever suffer, more intense pain than did Jesus on the cross. Think of the most awful, degrading, painful situation that you could suffer; take comfort that Jesus has suffered such pain. Corrie ten Boom, a Nazi concentration camp

prisoner, was comforted during the pain and dehumanizing degradation she suffered at the hands of her
guards. She bravely remembered Jesus. He hung naked
and vulnerable on the cross, enduring much worse pain
and humiliation than Miss ten Boom. Jesus despised the
cross, but drew strength from the joy that would later
come (Heb. 12:2).

Joni Eareckson Tada, injured in a diving accident,
compares her paralysis to the paralyzed condition of Jesus
while He was on the cross. He was quadriplegic—immo-
bile with no control over bodily functions. Jesus endured
all the pain and suffering we can imagine. Those strong
hands that once held the scepter of the universe were
nailed to a cross. "Consider him who endured such op-
position from sinful men, so that you will not grow weary
and lose heart" (Heb. 12:3).

When the sacrifice was complete, Jesus committed His
spirit into the hands of the Father. Now, according to
Scripture, Jesus sits at the right hand of the Father, a place
of power and honor. But, wait; there is an exception. The
Sanhedrin, pricked in their hearts with conviction, stoned
Stephen after he confronted them with the raw truth of
their disobedient and rebellious lives (Acts 7). Looking
into heaven, Stephen saw Jesus standing at the right hand
of God. Not sitting, but standing. In an expression of
grief and righteous indignation, Jesus stood with compassion and empathy for His dear friend Stephen. Jesus
was ready to receive this one who was persecuted and
accused falsely in His name. Stephen suffered death from
stoning at the hands of religious zealots. But he could
"rejoice and be glad" because he was going to be with
Jesus in heaven (Matt. 5:12).

Sitting or standing, Jesus, at the right hand of the
Father, is our advocate. "Who will bring any charge
against those whom God has chosen? It is God who jus-
tifies. Who is he that condemns? Christ Jesus, who died—
more than that, who was raised to life—is at the right

hand of God and is also interceding for us" (Rom. 8:33-34). We cannot be separated from Christ, and through Him we are more than conquerors.

Eager Hands

In the epilogue of Proverbs, King Lemuel's mother taught him (and us) the characteristics of a noble woman, and we still use them as a measure of virtue. She was trustworthy and energetic. She planned and prepared for her family, planted gardens, extended her charity outside her household to the poor, and sewed garments for her family and others. Never idle, she was always finding time for worship and praise of the Lord. The works of her hands brought her praise from her husband, her children, and even the public at the gates of the city (Prov. 31).

> I remember mother's hands.
> The brown age spots so hated by her.
> Her wedding rings,
> Tiny diamonds encircled with white gold;
> The only rings she ever wore.

> I remember Mother's hands.
> They cuddled me, scolded me, cooked for me.
> Her hand on my head soothed my fevered brow.
> Her hands sewed for me and pampered me.
> But most of all, they led me.

> I remember mother's hands
> The night she died.
> The angels came for her;
> With her hands, she reached for Jesus
> Forever to be at His side.

Betty Jo Lewis

Ministering Hands

Mary and Martha of Bethany, sisters and frequent hostesses of Jesus, had contrasting temperaments. But they both ministered with their hands. They lived with their brother, Lazarus, in a comfortable home not far from Jerusalem.

Martha was practical, perhaps older, and, in my opinion, of sanguine temperament because of her extrovertedness—hasty speech and actions. She spoke her mind. No one wondered what Martha might be thinking.

After Lazarus died and Jesus came too late, or so Martha thought, she was the first to meet Him and cry, "Lord, if you had been here, my brother would not have died. But I know that even now God will give you whatever you ask" (John 11:21-22).

Martha loved entertaining, especially if she could do everything just right. She was a woman of action and quick with any declaration of faith. Martha was the first to hear Jesus say, " 'I am the resurrection and the life. He who believes in me will live, even though he dies; and whoever lives and believes in me will never die. Do you believe this?'

'Yes, Lord,' she told him, 'I believe that you are the Christ, the Son of God, who was to come in the world' " (John 11:25-27).

Martha ministered with her hands by cooking, serving, and decorating a home, then sharing that home with friends, family, and perhaps even strangers. She could be curt and impatient if preparations were not on schedule or not going according to her plans.

Mary, on the other hand, was a melancholy introvert— quiet and sweet. Mary ministered with hands that were more likely to be folded in adoration and prayer as she sat at Jesus' feet. Someone has said that every time Mary is mentioned in the Scriptures, she is at the feet of Jesus. It was she who, with awesome sensitivity, poured the expensive ointment on His feet (John 11:1-2; 12:7). As if she

knew some things are worth dying for, there is no mention that Mary tried to dissuade Jesus from going to
Jerusalem. Jesus affirmed her action by referring to His
burial and the appropriate anointing of the body.

Mary's quiet soul and personality allowed her the
blessing of time at Jesus' feet, listening to spiritual truths.
She was mesmerized by His teaching and filled with adoration. Schedule and preparations had no hold on Mary
when she was in the presence of the Teacher.

Outspoken Martha and quiet, attentive Mary—two sisters with very different personalities, but both with hands
that ministered to Jesus. We need to remember the rebuke
the Lord gave Martha when she complained that Mary
wasted time in His presence. He gently told Martha that
Mary had made the right choice. Martha had allowed the
preparations to become a worry and bother to her.
" 'Martha, Martha,' the Lord answered, 'you are worried
and upset about many things, but only one thing is
needed. Mary has chosen what is better, and it will not be
taken away from her' " (Luke 10:38-42).

We can rejoice because housework is of temporal
value and we are cautioned it must not take precedence
over time spent with Jesus and His Word. I believe that
another implied lesson is that whatever our temperament,
our ministering hands must first be worshipping hands.

The Hands of Moses

The hand of God was on Moses from the beginning. His
mother, a brave, courageous, and creative woman, saved her
baby from the death knell of Pharaoh by hiding him in a boat
she fashioned from a papyrus basket. Placing the boat in the
river, she instructed Miriam, Moses' sister, to hide in the
bushes along the river near the place where the princess
came to bathe. Moses' mother hoped the princess would find
the baby and want him for her own. The princess did find the
baby and wanted to take him to the palace. Then, Miriam vol-
unteered her mother as a wet nurse for baby brother.

The real-life drama unfolded like a well-written script. Baby Moses was spared and he grew to young adulthood in the palace of Pharaoh. As a young man, however, Moses' hands got him into trouble. He was eyewitness to the beating of a Hebrew slave at the hand of an Egyptian. Filled with indignant rage and thinking no one was watching, Moses killed the Egyptian and hid the body in the sand. But Moses forgot about the slave who quickly spread the word of his rescue at the hand of the prince.

Fearing a death sentence, Moses fled to Midian. He became a shepherd, married, and probably gave up all thought of returning to Egypt. But God had not given up. He remembered His people, enslaved at the hands of the Egyptians.

One day God spoke to Moses through a burning bush in the desert. God divulged His rescue plan to Moses. A lengthy dialogue ensued between the two. Moses asked many skeptical questions. The final big question was: What if the Egyptians don't believe me? (Ex. 3-4).

"Then the Lord said to him, 'What is that in your hand?' 'A staff,' he replied.

The Lord said, 'Throw it on the ground' " (Ex. 4:2-3).

The rest of the story reminds us that whatever we hold in our hands can be God's tools of mercy, rescue, and compassion, or weapons of wrath. Whatever is in our hands can also be a barrier to our service and obedience to God. Like Moses, we must empty our hands and hold them open to God in worshipful abandonment. Then, He can place in them whatever we need to do the job He wants to do.

During Moses' ministry, his hands held the staff of God that delivered the Hebrews out of slavery, parted the waters for their escape, wrought the miracles and the plagues, and won military battles. With committed hands, Moses carried forth the mighty plan of God. And at the end of his life, he laid his hands on Joshua in blessing, giving him a spirit of wisdom (Deut. 34:9).

"For no one has ever shown the mighty power or performed the awesome deeds that Moses did in the sight of all Israel" (Deut. 34:12).

Hands of Paul

At the hands of the Apostle Paul, Christians were stoned, tents were made, churches were planted, and Biblical epistles that we read today were penned. Who can imagine an example more illustrative of blessing and curses at the hand of one man? Paul was indeed a violent man, but was shown mercy because he acted out of ignorance and unbelief. He called himself the worst of sinners (1 Tim. 1:13-16). In Paul's life we see the hope that is available for all of us, regardless of our background. When we say yes to Jesus, He virtually puts our hand in His and leads us through a productive, abundant life.

God sometimes chooses to work miracles with His own hands. More often it seems God's hands are our hands. Are we available? Are we usable clay in the Potter's hands? Are we ready to be His ministering hands in this hurting world?

CHAPTER THREE

Clay in the Potter's Hands

The encounter took place on the way to our room in the multistoried hotel which was host to 15,000 Acteens at the National Acteens Convention (NAC). The evening session had just ended. Girls and their laughter filled the lobby and every elevator. The one we took turned out to be the "milk run." On every floor the elevator stopped to deliver girls and take on more. The sweet encounter happened at one of the stops.

"Hey, I'm gonna be a missionary!" shrieked the excited Acteen.

"Home or foreign?" we responded through the six-inch opening of the elevator door, which closed before we heard her answer. It didn't matter. She had plenty of time to work out the details of her missions commitment. The immediate thrill was her enthusiasm for the mind-boggling thought: I am usable in God's hands.

The image of God's newest servant is imprinted on our hearts and minds. Praise God for her excitement. We pray for her as she matures in her missions commitment. We pray that as her missions awareness increases, so will her availability.

Perhaps the most amazing truth in all of the world is God desires and plans to work through people—you and me. God is certainly capable of supernaturally working in the world. But Jesus modeled the way God seems to prefer working—one on one. Jesus, being human, was mostly confined to one place. Part of Jesus' coming to earth was an emptying of Himself and accepting self-imposed limitations. With some exceptions, He operated in this fashion throughout His earthly ministry.

Who Is the Potter?

"But who are you, O man, to talk back to God? Shall what is formed say to him who formed it, 'Why did you make me like this?' Does not the potter have the right to make out of the same lump of clay some pottery for noble purposes and some for common use?" (Rom. 9:20-21).

The Potter is God, sovereign God, the creator and keeper of the universe. God is always at work. He did not stop working after the creation. He merely rested. And He is at work today in our world.

In John 5, Jesus is in trouble with the religious establishment because He healed a man on the Sabbath. Responding to the questioning Pharisees, Jesus claimed equality with the Father who is always working in this world to bring about His purpose and His plan.

Who Is the Clay?

Jesus willingly became clay in the Potter's (Father's) hands. He told the Pharisees, " 'My father is always at his work to this very day, and I, too, am working. The Son can do nothing by himself; he can do only what he sees his Father doing, because whatever the Father does the Son also does. For the Father loves the Son and shows him all he does' " (John 5:17, 19).

When a potter has clay in his hands or on the wheel, he is constantly working. The clay is pliable and moist. The potter shapes and molds the clay into valuable art or useful objects. If a foreign object gets into the clay, marring it, the clay is flawed. The potter breaks the flawed clay and remolds or reshapes the clay, or he casts it aside—unusable.

In Jeremiah 18, the Lord sent Jeremiah to see a potter and to learn a message for Israel: The nation of Israel
was chosen by Me. They are the people to carry out My
plans and purposes. But they are marred; they need to
be reshaped and remolded. The nation of Israel is
marred because of rebelliousness, stubbornness, and
disobedience.

Israel—the chosen ones of God, the ones who knew
God intimately—always had a better idea. Time and again
they had been delivered from the consequences of their
disobedience. Their mission in this world had worldwide
significance. But they had forsaken their first love.
Jeremiah wept as he witnessed their worship of false
gods, their burnt offerings, and the sacrifice of their own
flesh and blood. God was repulsed. Israel must be broken
and reshaped, remolded into what God intended.

Jeremiah warned the people, giving them the object
lesson of a marred pot and the potter. He offered them
the hope of God's promise that He would relent if they
would repent. He urged them to reform their ways.

The tragic response of the people is intolerable to
God. Why would they not repent? Why, in the face of
such promise and hope, did they choose hopelessness
and pursue impending doom?

The response is filled with pathos and woe and dis-
astrous consequences. I can imagine a black-bordered
document read with weeping and remorse: " 'It's no use.
We will continue with our own plans; each of us will follow the stubbornness of his evil heart' " (Jer. 18:12).

Their heart's cry could have been Isaiah 64:8. "Yet,
O Lord, you are our Father. We are the clay, you are
the potter; we are all the work of your hand. Do not
be angry beyond measure, O Lord; do not remember
our sins forever. Oh, look upon us, we pray, for we
are all your people."

Isaiah delivered strict woes to disobedient children:
"Woe to those who go to great depths to hide their plans

from the Lord, who do their work in darkness and think, 'Who will see us? Who will know?' You turn things upside down, as if the potter were thought to be like the clay! Shall what is formed say to him who formed it, 'He did not make me'? Can the pot say of the potter, 'He knows nothing' "? (Isa. 29:15-16).

And, "Woe to him who quarrels with his Maker, to him who is but a potsherd among the potsherds on the ground. Does the clay say to the potter, 'What are you making?' Does your work say, 'He has no hands'? Concerning things to come, do you question me about my children, or give me orders about the work of my hands?" (Isa. 45:9-11).

So flawed clay is broken and wasted, unusable, thrown out as garbage, heaped on the dump, never to fulfill its original destiny or purpose. But, people, unlike clay, have a choice. We may choose to be obedient and usable in God's hands. God's plan is for our hands to be His hands.

"Are we out of commission?" asks Avery Willis, vice-president for overseas operations for the Foreign Mission Board. "We are supposed to be people on mission under direct command from our Lord. What good is a toy, a tool, or any piece of equipment that is out of commission? No good. It is either thrown out or put on a shelf."

Lydia, Clay in the Potter's Hands

The Apostle Paul, on one of his missionary journeys in Troas, waited for leadership from the Lord before he continued his travels. He had been prevented by the Spirit of Jesus from going into Asia. One night Paul saw a vision of a man, pleading, "Come over to Macedonia and help us" (Acts 16:9b). Considering the vision to be the leadership of God, Paul and his companions immediately prepared for departure to Philippi and its major city, Macedonia.

On the Sabbath, Paul and his friends went to the river where they expected to find a place of prayer. Finding a group of women gathered, Paul began to share the gospel message with them. Lydia, a worshipper of God, responded to Paul's message of salvation through Jesus as "the Lord opened her heart" (Acts 16: 14b). So Lydia, a woman, became the first Christian in Europe (Acts 16).

Lydia was a business woman. Converted Lydia was hospitable, prayerful, and influential, and still a business woman. Her household, which consisted of family and perhaps employees, followed her in believer's baptism. She prayed for Paul and Silas while they were in jail and ministered to them upon their release.

Writing to those new Christians in Philippi, Paul admonished them to be faithful, assuring them God had begun the work in them and would be faithful to complete it. Paul joyfully thanked God for the Christians in Philippi, where Lydia was among the leaders. This was his prayer: "that your love may abound more and more in knowledge and depth of insight, so that you may be able to discern what is best and may be pure and blameless until the day of Christ, filled with the fruit of righteousness that comes through Jesus Christ—to the glory and praise of God" (Phil. 1:9).

Dorcas' Hands Ministered to the Poor

Dorcas may very well be called the virtuous woman of the New Testament. Acts 9:36 reminds us she was "always doing good and helping the poor." The hands of Dorcas were busy as a seamstress; even today there are Dorcas Sewing Societies all over the world.

Dorcas lived in the port city of Joppa, about 35 miles northwest of Jerusalem. Perhaps she saw the poor as they wandered along the beaches looking for rags which washed upon the seashore. Dorcas busied herself making proper garments for those needy people. Their new garments, made with her nimble fingers, gave them a new sense of self-respect. But Dorcas got sick and died.

Peter arrived in Joppa to find great mourning at the death of the beloved woman. The people rushed to tell him of her death and to show him the clothing she had made for them.

Peter sent them all from the room; after praying, he called her back from the dead then presented her alive and well to her friends. Some think that God enabled Peter to bring her back from death because of her ministry among the poor. The news of her resuscitation rippled throughout Joppa and many believed in the Lord. God uses those whose hands are committed to Him (Acts 9:36-43).

Priscilla, Aquila, and Apollos

The New Testament also introduces us to Priscilla, another beautiful example of clay in the Potter's hand. In their tent-making business, she and her husband, Aquila, interwove their business with their passion— teaching their faith to inquirers and converts. Two churches met in their homes; one in Corinth and one in Ephesus.

Perhaps one of the most significant contributions Priscilla made to the spreading of the gospel was recognizing that Apollos needed a deeper understanding of Christianity. Converted under the ministry of John the Baptist, Apollos came to Ephesus to speak. Priscilla and Aquila realized his need, invited him into their home, and "explained to him the way of God more adequately" (Acts 18:26).

Eunice and Lois, Godly Mother and Grandmother

Eunice and Lois, the mother and grandmother of Timothy, the well-known New Testament pastor, were also clay in the Potter's hand. They have no fame of their

own; instead they poured their life and faith into a little
boy who would grow to be such a fine Christian that the
Apostle Paul would count him as a dear friend and call
him "my dear son" (2 Tim. 1:2).

In fact, all we know of Eunice and Lois is contained
in one verse. Paul, writing to affirm Timothy's faith, said,
"I have been reminded of your sincere faith, which first
lived in your grandmother Lois and in your mother
Eunice" (2 Tim. 1:5).

The two women lived in Lystra; both were very involved in young Timothy's spiritual training. Perhaps
grandmother Lois kept Timothy while Eunice earned the
living. The investment of time and energy by the two
women underscores the importance of time and training
in a young child's life.

The crowning compliment for any Christian mother
and grandmother echoes off the pages of the New
Testament as Paul reaffirmed young Timothy in his faith.
"But as for you, continue in what you have learned and
have become convinced of, because you know those
from whom you learned it, and how from infancy you
have known the holy Scriptures, which are able to make
you wise for salvation through faith in Christ Jesus" (2
Tim. 3:14-15).

Of course, Timothy was not perfect, nor were Eunice
and Lois. Surely they experienced, as we do, days of
frustration and hours of hardship as well as times when
they didn't feel like successful laborers. I well remember
a lively discussion with my teenaged son, Mark. I'm not
quite sure of the topic but it had to do with my admonishing him not to do something.

"Mark, I'm just trying to keep you from learning the
hard way," I insisted.

To which he replied, "Mom, you know that's the only
way I ever learn anything."

Did Timothy ever say that? We don't know, but we
do know he was an assertive leader who left home and

loved ones at about the age of 15 to join Paul in planting the gospel around their world.

Eunice and Lois were faithful clay in the Potter's hand. He enabled them to mold the clay, young Timothy, with the strength and passion of the Potter, into an adult who "had known the Scriptures since infancy" (2 Tim. 3:15).

As faithful clay in the Potter's hands, we understand the urgency of ministry with children. They are innocent, blank slates who need loving adults to nurture them. They are children—handle with care.

Children—
Handle with Care

Three-year-old Emily sat listening to her daddy give the children's sermon one Sunday morning. She was one of several preschoolers gathered at his feet. Solemnly, Pastor Matt told them a story about when, as a little boy, he had been angry with a friend. The children listened wide-eyed as he described how he had said awful and untrue things about his friend. The pastor confessed that his motive had been to make the other boys dislike the friend with whom he was angry. But, much to his surprise, his friends turned against him instead of the intended victim. Then, Pastor Matt described his pitiful state of friendlessness, and the children tried to understand such an awful circumstance. Suddenly little Emily could stand it no longer, and she blurted, "But you had your mommy!" A tense second of silence was broken by laughter from the adults. The children's sermon was over.

But Emily was right—every boy and girl should have a daddy and a mommy! Every child needs a family. A television commercial for an adoption agency featured a little boy who said, "I just want someone to eat dinner with me, to check my homework, to play ball with me. I'd have someone if I had a family."

In God's plan every child is meant to have two parents and a safe and secure environment in which to grow and develop. The sinful human condition has thwarted God's original ideal. Christians, living according to God's plan, must make a difference in the lives of hurting children.

Jesus met the need of a multitude by using what one little boy placed in His hands (Matt. 15:29-39), and in doing so, He acknowledged the significance of a child. There were thousands of hungry people . . . one little boy . . . one lunch. The disciples were desperate when the thronging crowd grew restless. Tempers were ignited by growling stomachs. People were pushing and shoving to hear the words from the Teacher.

Crowds have a dehumanizing effect which can cause a sense of anonymity; and feeling anonymous is close to feeling nonexistent. Have you ever felt insignificant in a crowd? Perhaps the little boy with the lunch felt similar feelings. Maybe his initial reaction to the adults' request for his lunch was slow. Maybe the lad dallied as he contemplated giving up his lunch. We might imagine that the little boy first thought, "That's MY lunch," and clutched it to himself. Then imagine him reaching out to Jesus, handing Him the cherished lunch.

Later, after the crowd was filled with food and satisfied from their hunger, the quizzical child might have exclaimed, "That's NOT MY fish, MY bread!" But it was. After being placed in the hands of Jesus, the little boy's lunch blessed and satisfied thousands of people. The crowd had their immediate need met, but the disciples learned the complete sufficiency of the Savior.

What about our lunch? We can make a significant difference in a child's life by giving our lunch to Jesus. We must not hide in the crowd. We are gifted. Our spiritual gift is like a lunch we can place in the hands of Jesus. And our material wealth, time, and creative energy are resources Jesus is waiting to use.

Children Need Families

These are times when we must champion the family. The word family is being maligned and redefined today, and the maligning and redefining seem to have an insidious purpose—to salve the consciences of those who disagree with the Biblical model of family. Any astute observer of our nation since the 1950s must acknowledge the chaotic results. Any redefinition should be done by God; we have never improved on God's ideal of one man and one woman together for life, completing each other and parenting their offspring.

But God's plan for marriage and home lies in heaps. People have messed up, their lives askew with broken dreams and shattered hopes. Worst of all, children, the unintended victims of adult mistakes, are often abandoned or abused. But compassion without judgment, embodied in Christian women, can move in to restore, renew, and offer hope. You and I must be the hands of Jesus, ministering to neglected children. But first, we must hand our children to God.

Our Family, God's Family

Parents of preschool and school-age children must first devote their love and attention to their own children. Nurturing our children must be a priority. Motherhood is a high calling and demands energy, creativity, and organization.

"What is a family?" asks Edith Schaeffer in her book of the same title. She cleverly and beautifully compares the family to an ever-changing mobile, a real work of art. She describes the home as an environment that demands ecological balance for the growth of human beings. She considers the family an endangered species, and rejects the title housewife in favor of "Ecologist—in the most important area of conservation—the family."[1]

Christian families and homes are not meant to be cold, legalistic, perfect spheres where mistakes are hushed and hidden. Rather, they are to be warm lighthouses of unconditional love, bastions of forgiveness and acceptance, and schools of conflict resolution. We have the joy of modeling in our communities the complete and perfect love of Jesus in our imperfect families. And our homes must hand the truth of God to our children.

"What we have heard and known, what our fathers have told us. We will not hide them from their children; we will tell the next generation the praiseworthy deeds of the Lord, his power, and the wonders he has done. Then they would put their trust in God and would not forget his deeds but would keep his commands" (Psalm 78:3-4, 7).

A young mother with three little children in tow came to speak to Larry after he had preached a missions challenge in her church. (She reminded me of myself when our three children were less than four years of age.) Tearfully and sincerely, she declared her desire to "go do missions." He patiently listened to her while I observed from the sideline. In my heart I cried for her to see the mission field clinging and squirming around her feet. Reaching out and touching a lost world for Jesus does not mean neglecting one's own household. One's own home is a dignified and worthy place to be the hands of Jesus.

Our children need to experience hands-on ministry. They need to be involved in missions as well as to hear or read about missions. Children are capable of extending the hands of Jesus in ministry by using their own hands in such activities as packing sandwiches for feeding programs. Nursing homes are eager receivers of children with their crafts, music, and boundless energy. Involving your children in such activities and hands-on projects is an excellent way to teach as well as minister.

Years ago, on a cross-country family vacation, our oldest child engaged in a tract ministry. I don't think Janet missed one waitress, motel clerk, or fast-food restaurant. All were recipients of her printed gospel presentation. She enthusiastically shared her faith without ever knowing any results from her efforts.

Recently, newly appointed missionaries at a week of orientation for their work in partnership with the Home Mission Board, were curious about the brown paper bags at the front of the room. As Bill Graham, the director of Missionary Personnel department for the Home Mission Board, ended the session, he began passing out the bags, explaining that cookies were inside. Mission Friends from local churches made the cookies for the new missionaries. What a wonderful and early start in teaching the importance of missionary friendship and support.

Seeing the world through a child's eyes is refreshing and exciting. Investing time and love in a child's life when he or she may not otherwise receive such a precious gift is an investment with immeasurable dividends.

Many children today seem to be adrift in a sea of loneliness, spending blocks of time without the benefit of human interaction or adult supervision. Instead their "companions" are the miracles of modern technology—television, video games, compact discs, and portable radios.

A study reported on NBC's *Today* revealed that children who eat dinner with their families at least four times per week do better in school and have higher test scores. Can you remember when gathering the family for the dinner hour was the norm rather than the exception?

And often when all family members are at home, togetherness doesn't describe the situation. More aptly, the blaring television renders personal interaction impossible. We do have the power—we just need the will—to turn off the televisions. We need to read more, both collectively and individually. We need more family conversation, a declining art which edifies and stimulates each family member.

We need to slow our pace of life. Children need time to be children. There is only a small window of opportunity to nurture them as children. One day in the grocery store, I was amused to hear a small voice pleading, "Slow down, Mommy, slow down." I looked to see a wiry five-year-old double-stepping to keep pace with his harried mom. Her rush symbolized the intensive pace we live today.

The average face-to-face conversation time spent between fathers and young sons is reported to be 37 seconds per day. If that is true, fathers must be raising strangers. The father needs to be present in the home emotionally and intellectually as well as physically.

Children need relaxed downtime as well as time and interaction with their parents. Lessons for children from karate to ballet and involvement in sports develop their

character and sharpen skills. But too much activity pro-
duces stress and robs the children from their childhood
and the family of precious time together, relating to
each other. It is encouraging to see young parents in
our churches devising new family systems that throw
out traditional paradigms, yet bring honor to God and
His Word.

The *Shema*

"Hear, O Israel: The Lord our God, the Lord is one. Love
the Lord your God with all your heart and with all your
soul and with all your strength. These commandments
that I give you today are to be upon your hearts. Impress
them on your children. Talk about them when you sit at
home and when you walk along the road, when you lie
down and when you get up. Tie them as symbols on
your hands and bind them on your foreheads. Write
them on the doorframes of your houses and on your
gates" (Deut. 6:4-9).

A hint for home decorating is even included in the
Shema—to write the statutes of the Lord on our doorframes. Years ago, when we moved to Pennsylvania, we
bought our house from a Jewish family. They had placed
a small brass scroll on the front doorframe, symbolizing
the law of Moses. Each time family members passed
through the door, they touched the scroll with their hand
and recited the blessing, "May you reenter in the same
condition as you leave." Maybe this was not exactly what
the Deuteronomy passage instructs, yet a nice tradition.

I, and many of my Christian friends, can testify of having grown up in homes where even the walls preached
the gospel. Lovely framed Scripture passages and
Christian mottoes extended a gospel witness to all who
came into our homes and also reminded the inhabitants
of God's precepts.

Gentiles do well to heed the God-given Jewish formula
for family religious instruction—to teach our children as

we sit in our homes, when we walk by the way, and when we lie down and rise up. How can our children be taught in this manner if we never sit together, eat together, take walks together, enjoy events together, pray together, or close the day together at bedtime?

Indeed, the first step in ministering to children is to take care of your own, giving of yourself freely to their nurturing and development. It is also good for a mother to involve her own children in ministry to others, meeting the needs of less fortunate children.

There Is Weeping for the Children

"A voice is heard in Ramah, mourning and great weeping, Rachel weeping for her children and refusing to be comforted, because her children are no more" (Jer. 31:15). Our nation is saturated with tears for the children. There is weeping for kidnapped children, for children killed in cross fire or drive-by shootings, for molested children, for children who are victims of incest. There is weeping for children starved for food as well as emotional nutrition.

The state of American's children has been called "a quiet crisis." Consider these facts:
- American children are more likely to be poor, drug-dependent, pregnant, murdered, or incarcerated than children in any other industrialized nation.
- Nearly 70 percent of all child-care workers earn less than the average parking lot attendant.
- One-fourth of all births in the United States today are to unwed mothers.
- One-fourth of American children under age three live in families with incomes below the federal poverty level.
- In the United States, nine of every 1,000 infants die before they reach their first birthday—a mortality rate higher than that of 19 other nations.
- Most US kids spend three hours or more a day sitting passively in front of the television.
- Teen suicides have tripled in the past 30 years.[2]

The "quiet crisis" analogy doesn't always fit. The crisis is noisy and deafening in the places where children group in gangs to seek self-esteem for themselves and to wreak havoc on anyone who gets in their way. Negligence toward these children results in a thunderous reverberation.

Children, our nation's greatest natural resource, are powerless in their own behalf. But the weeping and the clamor is being heard by caring and compassionate Christians. We all must take action. Jesus wants to touch troubled children with our hands. The children we reach today are the laborers in the Lord's vineyard tomorrow.

Our churches must answer the alarming cry and engage in ministry to children as Christ would do if He were physically here. Churches today can be yesterday's extended family. Crossing generational lines as we group for church suppers, classes, and other gatherings is an innovative way to mix age groups. A good plan might be for everybody to adopt somebody.

All Children Deserve a Helping Hand

Literacy is the backbone of adult independence. Too often, children are passed through the school system without mastering basic skills. Then they quit school or graduate without functional literary skills. Without these skills, they most likely will become dependent adults and gloomy statistics.

People who can't read miss out on many of life's opportunities. Seventy-five percent of the unemployed, 33 percent of mothers receiving Aid to Families with Dependent Children, 60 percent of prison inmates, and 85 percent of juvenile offenders are functionally illiterate.[3]

Identifying and correcting reading disabilities early saves children from imminent failure. Remedial classes help, but the best solution is volunteers, working one-on-one with young children until their reading skills improve.

A nonreading future for a child is grim. They face the possibility of becoming a criminal or a victim, as well as a dependent person. Nonreaders sometimes lash out in anger toward a system that has grossly failed them, or they languish through their adult existence searching for significance.

When parents are unavailable, other adults need to fill the gap. Volunteer in a neighborhood school, at church, or in the children's home, or get involved in the legislative process in your county and state. Connect with a child to provide the love and nurturing that is otherwise missed. Families with a mother and father can "adopt" families with single mothers or fathers. This way, at play, at a meal, during prayer, or in worship, the children of single parents are exposed to both the male and female model that is missing from their lives. Natural, everyday problems are lived through and dealt with. Good conduct and problem-solving techniques are caught as well as taught. Everyone feels love and acceptance.

Let the Children Come unto Me

" 'See that you do not look down on one of these little ones. For I tell you that their angels in heaven always see the face of my Father in heaven' " (Matt. 18:10). Jesus set the example for us. He handled children with care. With compassion, Jesus cast the evil spirits from a demoniac boy, restoring a father's only son (Luke 9). Jesus took time to go to Jairus' house and restore life to his little girl (Mark 5). To the Canaanite woman who pled for her daughter's healing from evil spirits, Jesus granted her request (Matthew 15). We must be intercessors, faithfully praying for hurting and angry children.

Children were important to Jesus. He demonstrated genuine appreciation for their personhood. He compared being saved to becoming like a little child. How does one become like a little child? As Nicodemus asked, do we reenter our mother's womb and start all over (John 3)? Becoming like a child involves recognizing our need and dependence. Picture a little child asking, "Daddy, will you . . . ?" This is what relating to Jesus as a child is like. We become as children who believe and trust authority.

Adults can be too self-reliant and carry a lot of extra baggage in terms of painful memories, feelings, and emotions. It's easy for a little child to trust daddy "to fix it." Children innocently receive Jesus.

Who Is Greatest in the Kingdom?

Jesus and His disciples had reached Capernaum when He inquired about an argument the disciples had on the way. The embarrassed disciples were reluctant to answer Him. They were afraid because their argument had been about who would be the greatest in the kingdom (Mark 9:33-37).

Can you imagine asking Jesus who is greatest in His kingdom? Jesus' answer reveals His love and concern for children as well as the disciples. They discussed their troubling debate. And they learned whoever wanted to be the greatest or first had to be the last, the servant of all. But most of all, they learned their argument was superfluous and a distraction to their usefulness in the kingdom.

Jesus sat down and used a child to demonstrate His lesson. He stood the child in their midst. Then He hugged the child and told the disciples that whoever welcomes a little child in the name of Jesus welcomes Jesus, and whoever welcomes Jesus is really welcoming the Father who sent Jesus. He severely judged those who hinder children in any way from believing in Him. People brought little children to Jesus. They wanted Him to touch them. The disciples, viewing the children as a bother, as stumbling blocks which prevented the disciples from accomplishing their great deeds for the kingdom, rebuked the people. Children were of little significance in the big picture—the ambitious plans of the disciples.

Jesus did not rebuke the people; He rebuked the disciples. He instructed the disciples to let the little children come to Him and not to hinder them in any way, because the kingdom of God belongs to such as these. Taking the children into His arms, He placed His hands on them and blessed them. The kingdom of God is made up of people with childlike qualities (Mark 10:13-16).

The young David manifested his faith in the God of Israel when he went up against the Philistine giant, Goliath. The boy was victorious as he declared his strength "in the name of the Lord Almighty, the God of the armies of Israel, whom you [Goliath] have defied" (1 Sam. 17:45*b*). I can imagine that David wished many times for his childhood faith and innocence as he faced temptations in his adult life. Reflecting on the majesty of God, the psalmist David declared "from the lips of children and infants you have ordained praise" (Psalm 8:2*a*). After Jesus cleansed the temple and healed the blind and lame, the children at the temple shouted, "Hosanna to the Son of David." Jesus reminded the indignant chief priests of the words of Psalm 8 (Matt. 21:12-16).

I remember the first Christmas season that Larry was pastor of Tower Grove Baptist Church in St. Louis, Missouri. The congregation was gathered in the darkened sanctuary anticipating the children's choir presentation. The children, dressed in their angelic white frocks with floppy red bows, eagerly waited to process down the isle singing "O Come, All Ye Faithful." Our four-year-old Christy was in the choir. My composure unraveled at my first glimpse of her—bouncy, blonde curls surrounding a radiant face, little mouth in a perfect "O." What a beautiful sight—my four-year-old praising Jesus!

Pray for the Children

"Arise, cry out in the night, as the watches of the night begin; pour out your heart like water in the presence of the Lord. Lift up your hands to him for the lives of your children" (Lam. 2:19). In communities across the nation, groups of women are meeting regularly to pray for their children, teachers, and neighborhood school staffs. They pour out their concern, their fear, and their praise in intercession before the Lord. Victories of answered prayer wait on more and more groups to gather in prayer for the children.

Some adults are selfish and hopeless. Their solution for their own problems, or for the children they consider to be problems, is to snuff out their lives. They become so desperate that their warped reasoning gives them permission to eliminate their children. It is shocking, but not rare, to hear of parents killing their children. According to James Fox, a criminologist quoted in *USA Today*, "There are three cases a week in the United States where children under age 5 are killed by their mothers."[4]

One answer to the wanton murder of children is to seek an end to the isolation of families. Experts have observed that most murdered children are invisible to their communities, hidden inside their homes by the antisocial behavior of their caregivers. Relatives, neighbors, or friends, especially alert and concerned Christians, are the nearest answer. Observing isolation of children and family members, then responding with hospitality and offering friendship and assistance, might save a child's life.

A Census Bureau study reveals that 1.6 million children, ages 5 to 14 are home alone each day from the time school is out until a parent returns from work. Of these 1.6 million children, 500,000 are under age 12.[5] Without supervision and guidance, these children are left to fend for themselves. Some do quite well, while others suffer physical injuries or emotional depravation.

Loose the Chains of Injustice

"Loose the chains of injustice and untie the cords of the yoke, to set the oppressed free and break every yoke" (Isa. 58:6b). Surely the most insidious yoke children face is abuse at the hands of a caregiver, a trusted relative, or a predatory stranger.

Many children are victims of anonymous violence. Chains of injustice bind too many children in our nation. There is more child abuse, sexual and physical, today than in any other time.

Who are the abusers? They may be our friends, neighbors, or relatives. They are ordinary people who feel trapped in circumstances they cannot or do not know how to handle. People from every economic, racial, social, ethnic, and religious group are included in this depraved behavior.

Why does it happen? Abusive parents may feel socially isolated, have unmet emotional needs, lack parenting skills/knowledge, have a drug or alcohol problem, believe that violence or physical force is an accepted problem-solving method, or most often, have been abused themselves. Child abuse is a vicious cycle of the abused growing up to become the abuser.

The incredulous fact is that abused children usually feel at fault in these circumstances. Remember, the nature of a child is to trust authority. So when the trusted adult, or person in position of power, brings pain and shame into their lives, the children feel responsible. This feeling of responsibility and blame is as emotionally binding as a metal chain literally wrapped around their little bodies. The guilt and shame is carried into their adult lives and sometimes the victims become the perpetrators.

What is child abuse? The spectrum of child abuse includes the willful exploitation of a child for the sexual gratification of an adult, as well as harsh words or actions by an adult, that send an emotionally hurtful message to the child. It involves any nonaccidental physical injury as well as neglecting the physical, emotional, or medical needs of a child.

Physical, sexual, and emotional abuse of children is rampant. Out of 586 Southern Baptist adults who anonymously answered a questionnaire at the 1993 Southern Baptist Convention, one of every three had been sexually abused before the age of 18, and of those, every seven were incest victims. Forty-five percent of the women had one or more abusive experiences while 22 percent of men had one or more experience.[6]

Churches need to exercise caution in hiring children's workers. Extreme care must be taken in the interview process and in the checking of references. There should be a probationary period of employment before an employee is considered permanent. The criminal court clerk's office in the local county may offer advice and references. Local law enforcement officers have access to the nationwide files of the Federal Bureau of Investigation. Ask them to check a prospective employee or give advice to help the church avoid employing the wrong person.

Thousands of loving and dedicated people work with our children. We are so grateful for gifted children's workers. But the exceptions bring heartache and pain into our lives and bind our nation's children with unjust chains.[7]

A counselor in a protective shelter asked a sexually abused child to name her one desire. "To have someone love me, to cuddle and hold me," she replied.[8]

Another form of abuse to the children is rampant violence in the streets. Some live in such violent neighborhoods, they wait for the "bullet with their name on it." A little boy tearfully pleads to play outside, but "outside is too dangerous." Another accepts his violent fate with, "it ain't-a never gonna stop."

But violence is a two-sided coin. Children are often the perpetrators as well as the victims. On any given day, 90,000 juveniles are locked up in the United States. And the young people give lame reasons for their crimes such as:

"It gave me love and praise." (Being part of a group.)

"We could never fail, we could always accomplish crime."

"I'd never get caught."

"I never met my father."

"My anger started when I was eleven and my parents divorced."

Experts remind us we must offer violent children connection, purpose of life, a reason for existence and for hope, and a safety valve for anger. All too often we hear in the rehabilitation rooms of prisons, "I didn't have anyone to care about me." That is how children get to the point of not caring what they do to others.

On an August day in 1994, Ron Climer, church and community missionary in Fresno, California, visited the Fresno County juvenile maximum security detention center where he serves as chaplain. In the facility there are more juveniles than adults locked up for murder, and all the murders are drug and gang related. Ron read the following poem to 250 boys and girls, ranging in age from 8 to 18.

The Heavy Badge

Lord, I'm scared; Please hear my plea.
Please come and comfort me.
I just met a kid packing a gun.
He was shooting at people just for fun.
When he saw me, I saw fear, not fun,
For he saw I carried a badge and a gun.
I thought he would stop when I said
"Drop the gun."
Or maybe he'd turn on his heel and run.
But I watch in fear as his muzzle raised,
And I knew one of us was going to his grave.
I heard the sound of the muzzle blast,
And I held his head as he breathed his last.
The hurt and pain I feel in my heart,
Dear God, I think will tear me apart.
What did I do that was wrong today,
Could I have approached it from another way?
He seemed so young and angry with his life.
This guilt I feel cuts like a knife.
They tell me I shot in self defense,
That he was high and had no sense.
But somewhere there's a mother who's in terrible pain,
She will never see her child again.
Lord console her in her time of grief,
And for me, Please Lord, some blessed relief.
For this badge I wear carries a heavy price,
Today it was a young man's life.[9]

Missionary Ron correctly states, "Everyone on both sides of this war on crime is in desperate need of Jesus. In fact, if any positive results are to occur, it will only be by His presence."

This is not an "us versus them" situation. This is not an inner city versus suburban problem. Children's advocacy is about all of us and the solution lies in all Christians doing something about it.

I heard about a 12-year-old boy who went on a climb with his professional mountain-climbing mother. Together, they scaled a peak she judged would be reachable for him. At the apex, he stood proudly and announced, "Hey, Mom, I'm standing on top of my fears." May all children, through the nurturing protection of adults, be able to stand on their fears. "For God did not give us a spirit of timidity [fear], but a spirit of power, of love and of self-discipline" (2 Tim. 1:7).

Emily, pastor Matt's daughter, is cherished and precious to her parents, grandparents, and church family. She could not fathom the picture of abandonment her dad described. She could not imagine life without a loving, caring parent and the safe shelter of home. After all, to Emily, home is a refuge where mommy and daddy heal all hurts.

But, today, more than ever, home and family for many children does not mean loving parents providing a safe and secure environment. Instead, abused and exploited women who may be poor or emotionally deficient head many households. Their homes lack the basic ingredients of a safe and secure environment for themselves and their children.

Hand in Hand with Women

"Then the Lord God made a woman" (Gen. 2:22*a*). Maybe you have seen this familiar adage on refrigerator magnets, bumper stickers, or framed as cross-stitched art: "God couldn't be everywhere, so He made mothers." Though it is theologically unsound, the statement collaborates the idea of God using human hands to do His work. God empowers Christian women to nurture, care for, and minister to others.

Earlier we noted that God doesn't have physical hands. God is all powerful with all authority in His sovereign reign. However, He has chosen to work through the hands of people in ministry rather than sweeping a celestial wand over the details and areas of our lives. God is a God of order.

The Heavenly Father has chosen to allow the creation to operate according to its design and preset fashion through cause and effect. We are not earthly robots working at the bidding of a cosmic command center. Sovereign love allows for human choice. When intervention happens, and God does intervene, it is called a miracle. But more often, God does His work through people, allowing us to partake in the joy of being His hands in our world.

God began with an intentional purpose for women in the creation. Women are like integral pieces in a puzzle; they complete the picture. In God's ideal plan, men and women are of equal worth with complementary functions.

Jesus' thinking never conformed to the attitudes and customs toward women of His day. Time and again Jesus

affirmed women, their role, and their personhood. There is
not one incident in Scripture of God sanctioning a put-
down of women or making women second-class kingdom
citizens. Jehovah God of the Old Testament heard and answered the prayers of women, worked through the lives of
women, and performed miracles for women. Judgment of
sin happened in the lives of women, just as in the lives of
men. When women were sinned against, God came to
them in comfort. Women, like men, are pictured in reality
as sinners and can disturb God's plan or become God's
heroines.

Jesus continues the thread of acceptance, affirmation,
and availability to women in the New Testament. Women
ministered to Jesus and enhanced His ministry to people.
There is no evidence to support this, but I like to think
that the women who traveled with Jesus in His public
ministry may have been related to the disciples, perhaps
their wives and children. In that case, the children,
thought by the disciples to be a bother to Jesus on various occasions, could have been their very own. Single
women, probably part of the entourage, contributed sig-
nificantly to the needs of the group and found security
and protection in the family groupings.

The role of women in Scripture enhances and encourages
women of the present century to get involved, to minister. My
deep conviction is that God desires unhindered opportunity
for women. There is certainly no dispute as to the amount of
ministry or work to be done. Throughout the Scriptures
women ministered to men, children, and other women.

"It's the way we were raised!" cried my friend. We were
discussing the plight of women and trying to figure out why
so many women today have emotional problems. But the
problem is much older than the way we were raised. It orig-
inates with Eve and her sin—disobedience and discontent-
ment. Eve took her eyes off what she had and gazed
longingly on that which she was not allowed to have. Her
sin brought to her life and ours a warped understanding of

fulfillment. Women (and men) tend to look to the wrong things to satisfy the longing of their hearts. The ultimate answer is a right relationship with God through Christ.

The imbalances and injustices women face today may be the direct result of something in their past leading to emotional upheaval. But there is hope; there is healing. Learning to view their lives and purposes from God's perspective is liberating for women.

Society and culture affect women today as in the days of Jesus' earthly ministry. But true liberation, found in personal relationship with Jesus Christ, is the same then and now. Today the equality of women is touted as if we have come miles from the archaic days of Scripture. That day is disdained while today's liberation is paraded as a more exemplary model. But a closer look reveals that much work is needed today in truly liberating women's spirits, minds, and bodies. Satan is still deluding women and using men to perpetuate bondage while satisfying their own sensual, sinful desires. The incident in Scripture of the woman taken in adultery speaks to the timeless sinful nature of man to oppress women (see John 8). This warring faction between the sexes is the inevitable result of our sinful human nature. The ugliness of sin is manifested by the awful competition between the two sexes that were created to complement each other; they respect and complement each other more often when redeemed and rightly related to the Savior.

From the Beginning

Let's take a look at where it all began. God, the Creator, designed and brought into being a beautiful planet. He placed animal and plant life in balance, blending beauty and order.

Into this balanced beauty, He introduced a caretaker, man. The man delighted in his caretaking chores. He must have occupied himself for hours every day observing and becoming familiar with plant and animal behaviors. I imagine hours of delight as the earth's only man named the animals. Did he giggle at the sight of some of them? Did he tremble at the sight of others? Such wonder and beauty meshed in the perfectly ordered world without chaotic sin. Every part of creation was doing what it was created to do—no more, no less.

But a problem surfaces. Adam, as he was later called, noticed that all of creation had a counterpart. The animals came in pairs. Even the plant life had complementary parts, which resulted in reproduction if not companionship.

The first man felt a sense of isolation. He was grateful for his relationship to his Creator, but something was missing. There was no other like him. No counterpart for companionship. No one with whom to share joys. No one else with whom to wonder and marvel. No one else to match his intelligence and ability to think.

So he watched for a companion. Maybe she would appear in the long line of animals that he was naming. But it didn't happen. There was just no suitable helper for the man. Then he fell asleep. God knew the man's longing. The Creator waited for the man to know—to identify his incompleteness. The time had come. God would satisfy the man's heart desire—He would give man a woman. While the man was unconscious, the Creator (Father, Son, and Spirit) went to work. Hovering over him, They took a rib from Adam and formed another human being, a companion, a woman.

Adam woke up. "Wow!" he exclaimed. "She's here!" The Creator had surpassed all of Adam's expectations for a partner. He immediately recognized her likeness to him and his reaction is the first love poem. "This is bone of my bones and flesh of my flesh; she shall be called woman, for she was taken out of man" (Gen. 2:23). From the beginning to this very moment, God's original plan is still intact. Every normal man everywhere shares Adam's desire for female companionship, and woman still gives man a sense of completeness.

And so, women are special—a special creation with a special purpose and a special place in the sovereign scheme of God. Woman was given to man as a gift. She was not an afterthought. In God's sense of timing, Adam needed to know he needed her. And only then did God present her to Adam.

From the beginning, the man and woman basked in the friendship and companionship that was instantly theirs. Being a couple was extremely important. So much so that the Scriptures seem to jump ahead and interrupt the story in declaring, "For this reason a man will leave his father and mother and be united to his wife, and they will become one flesh" (Gen. 2:24).

They shared fellowship with each other and with God. Their work was pleasurable and without toil. Their relationship was untainted and pure. The Bible speaks of their being naked without shame. I believe much more than physical nakedness was implied. Each one's emotions were exposed to the other in complete openness and harmony of spirit, soul, and mind. They had a level of integrity in their relationship for which we can only wish today.

Days and nights were delightful search-and-discovery missions throughout their perfect habitat. Man and woman, completely equal in worth and complementary in function, lived in a place of perfect beauty and orderly fashion. In their utopian world, however, there were rules and boundaries. Both the man and the woman knew the rules.

The serpent, knowing Eve was vulnerable, deceived her. She partook of the forbidden fruit. One rule was broken—and everything was broken—their relationship to God, to each other, and to their physical world. What followed was an ugly portrayal of the blame game. Man blamed woman, woman blamed the serpent, both blamed circumstances. Both were a miserable failure.

But God did not abandon them. He had a plan. The Father sought His children to fix their brokenness. God searched for them in the garden, not because He didn't know where Adam and Eve were, but so they would comprehend their lostness. Always the initiator, merciful God yearned to mend the relationship—to give them a way out of the ugly circumstances of disobedience and rebellion. But there were consequences.

Eve was told that Adam would "rule over [her]" (Gen. 3:16b). This rule was a distinct difference in the circumstances of their relationship before their sin. The woman would not only experience pain in birthing her children (an unknown for Eve), but also a deep desire for her husband. What had changed? Had she not deeply desired her husband? Yes, but in their pre-sin condition, they enjoyed an emotional level of relationship that is incomprehensible to most couples today.

The breakdown in communication that befalls us—the barrier between the sexes—stems from each one's selfishness and causes much pain between males and females. A lack-of-trust wall was built up between Adam and Eve. A knowledge of self was lived out in selfishness rather than a generous giving of self to the other. So, the special creature, woman, though precious to God, is marred by sin. But God is so good. His agape love includes a plan of redemption for every man, woman, and child. This plan is not only a way of salvation and restoration to the pure fellowship of friendship through all eternity for the people, but also a plan to accomplish the mission of God on earth.

God's Design for Women

Elizabeth Elliot has written, "We are called to be women. The fact that I am a woman does not make me a different kind of Christian, but the fact that I am Christian does make me a different kind of woman. For I have accepted God's idea of me, and my whole life is an offering back to Him of all that I am and all that He wants me to be."[1]

The Creator gave women a special purpose in His plan. He equipped women with nurturing instincts, intuition, and sensitivity radar. Women are gifted by the heavenly Father with a capacity to love the lovely as well as the unlovely.

The female body is equipped to bear children. Woman's sin brought the reality of pain into this function. Certainly, not all women will or can bear children. But all women, sub-mitted to God in Christ, will know the pain of birthing spir-itual children into God's kingdom. The process of growing and nurturing spiritual children is not only one of blessed fulfillment, but the travail of accompanying joys and sorrows is akin to natural, physical motherhood.

Joyful is the woman who acknowledges her role in God's plan—who can resonate Mary's commitment to the angel, " 'I am the Lord's servant. . . . May it be to me as you have said' " (Luke 1:38a).

Known by God

Hagar, the Egyptian maidservant of Sarai, Abram's wife, min-istered to Sarai's daily physical needs. Of all Sarai's servants, Hagar was the most trusted. Perhaps that was the reason Sarai suggested to Abram that he take Hagar as a secondary wife (Gen. 16:2-3). Sarai, evidently concluding she was at fault because the promised child had not been born to her and Abram, suggested to Abram that he take Hagar as a wife and the two of them would conceive the promised child.

All was well until pregnant Hagar began to despise Sarai. Her hatred was returned by Sarai, who mistreated Hagar. Attempting to escape, perhaps to Egypt, Hagar fled into the wilderness.

An angel of the Lord confronted Hagar in the wilderness. " 'Hagar, servant of Sarai, where have you come from, and where are you going?' " (Gen. 16:8).

The philosophical question asked of Hagar is one every person faces. Jesus modeled the answer in John's Gospel for us: " 'I am the way and the truth and the life' " (John 14:6a).

Before He demonstrated servanthood by washing His disciples' feet, the Scriptures declare "Jesus knew that the Father had put all things under his power, and that he had come from God and was returning to God" (John 13:3). Jesus knew where He came from and where He was going.

An important principle for a meaningful life of ministry and outreach to others is the knowledge of one's source as

well as goal. A prerequisite for effective ministry is focus and
direction that comes with a surrender to Jesus Christ as our
Lord, and acknowledgment that He is our source, guide, and
goal. "For from him (our source) and through him (our
guide) and to him (our goal) are all things" (Rom. 11:36a).[2]

So, Hagar was asked life's most important question. But
Hagar didn't have the New Testament to help her answer. She
simply stated her present circumstance, "I'm running away
from my mistress Sarai" (Gen. 16:8b). Hagar was admonished
by the angel of the Lord to return and submit to her mistress.

Hagar obeyed, but she was a different Hagar. She had
a purpose, a reason for being. Genesis 16:13 reveals that
Hagar's confrontation with God had given her an identity. Even though her circumstances were the same—and
certainly less than ideal—Hagar had the strength to return to Sarai and minister to her and the household. The
ministering hands of God on Sarah were in the form of
an Egyptian servant girl who knew God and also knew
she was known by Jehovah God. "'You are the God who
sees me, for she said, I have now seen the One who sees
me' " (Gen. 16:13b).

Woman to Woman

We've already established the fact that women are a special
creation and have a special place and purpose in God's
overall design. Part of the uniqueness of womanhood includes sisterhood. Women share an identity, a binding of
spirits, an affinity. Women need each other and thrive on intimate woman-to-woman friendships.

A recent study by the Home Mission Board's Research
Division revealed startling facts concerning women in the
United States. One of the most telling statistics concerned
anger among women. Not only are large numbers of women
angry, but their anger is directed at men. Most angry women
are furious with men in general because of their relationships with men in particular. They have suffered at the
hands of abusive fathers, husbands, or male employers. One

woman in counseling said, "Every man in my life has either walked out on me, used me, or abandoned me." It is a tragedy that affects all of us when a woman has never been in a relationship with a man who holds her in high esteem.

The conclusion of the study suggests an urgent task in evangelism for Christian women. Who can best minister to the angry female segment of our population? A Christian man or woman? The sovereignty of God notwithstanding, it is logical to assume angry women may best be led into a personal relationship to Jesus Christ by other women.

Operation Lydia, which originated in Detroit, Michigan, is a unique approach to church planting using women's Bible study groups. Doc and Holly Lindsey, former missionaries in Detroit and now in Wisconsin-Minnesota, found that women can effectively start and lead these groups. They are better able to move in and out of turf and drug zones with relative safety because they are women. Dr. Raymond Bakke, the director of International Urban Associates in Chicago, Illinois, has said, "Some places are so dangerous, only a woman can go."

Women Need Women

Women need each other, and all women need the Lord. Here are some startling statistics from *Women 1994,* the fourth annual report on women through the Women's Department of the Baptist World Alliance.[3]

- Global Conditions—The global situation for women is getting worse. Economic recession hurts women first and worst. Political upheaval, often resulting in war, turns women into victims. Religious trends are repressing women. The world's fastest growing religion is Islam—traditionally anti-woman.

- Population—The percentage of females in the general population continues to decline (now standing at just under 49.6 percent). This is due to erosion of women's health, to deaths in childbirth, to selective abortion of females, to murder of women.

- Teenage Pregnancy—A growing percentage of the world's births is due to teenage pregnancy. This is true not only in developing nations where girls are married off in childhood, but also in developed nations where unsupervised teenaged girls conceive out of wedlock.
- Missing women—World population counts cannot find about 60 million women. Some United Nations reports indicate that the number missing is 100 million. These have been eliminated by selective abortion of female fetuses, female infanticide, and abuse of girls and women.
- Anemia—More than half of all pregnant women suffer from anemia. One-third of all nonpregnant women of reproductive age are anemic. This is a major contributor to the 500,000 maternal deaths due to complicated pregnancy and childbirth.
- AIDS—During the 1990s, the number of women and children dying of AIDS (and AIDS related causes) will rise to 3 million per year. Over 90 percent of women currently infected with HIV have been infected through intercourse, most of them by husbands.
- Depression—Forty percent of American women report being severely depressed, compared with 26 percent of men. Women under age 45 are more likely to experience depression than older women.
- Literacy and Education—Women continue to make up two-thirds of the world's illiterates.
- Migration and Immigration—Nearly half the migrants who cross international borders are women. In Europe, most foreign-born persons are female. Women constitute up to 75 percent of refugees. Women migrants are typically very young or very old.
- Violence—Most countries are reporting an increase in reported violence by men against women that results in injury or death. There is no reliable analysis of causes for this situation; whether there is an actual increase or whether customary violence is just now being reported.

Responding to these dire needs, the Women's Department of the Baptist World Alliance adopted a Proclamation of Good News for Women:

The Gospel of Jesus Christ is Good News to all the women of the world.
To those who are weighed down with guilt, it is forgiveness.
To those who sin, it is redemption and renewal.
To those who are oppressed, it is freedom.
To those who live in fear, it is peace.
To those who are despised and rejected, it is kinship with the God who endured the shame of the cross.
To those who are bound by culture and tradition it is emancipation by One who treated women as equals.
To those who cannot trust, it is dependence upon One who has shown himself trustworthy.
To those who are lonely, it is friendship with the Best Friend women ever had.
To those who are devalued, it is a new identity as joint-heirs of the grace of God.
As women who follow the Lord Jesus Christ, we are compelled by His love, commanded by His Word, and gifted by His Spirit to share this Gospel with those who have not seen or heard the salvation of our God.

Therefore, We will radiate His light into the dark corners of women's experience;
We will bear His life to those who are dying;
We will share our bread with those who are hungry;
We will declare His promise of resurrection to those who have no hope;
We will proclaim His empowerment to those who are powerless;
We will bring affirmation to those who do not know they are made in the image of God.
We will see with the eyes of Jesus, weep with His tears, hear with His ears, speak with His words, touch with His hands, embrace with His arms, and feel with His heart

Until that great day comes when every woman, man, and child
will know the glorious grace and goodness of our God.[4]

Women Mentoring Women

The Scriptures are replete with models of women mentoring women. Some of them are relatives and some
friends: Naomi and Ruth, Lois and Eunice, Mary and
Martha, Elizabeth and Mary, Jochebed and Miriam. Other
women who doubtlessly were mentors among their
friends and households are Esther, Dorcas, Lydia, Priscilla,
and Phoebe. The Apostle Paul, leaving Titus on the island
of Crete to finish the discipling and church strengthening,
instructed Titus to use women to teach women.
"Likewise, teach the older women to be reverent in the
way they live, not to be slanderers or addicted to much
wine, but to teach what is good. Then they can train the
younger women to love their husbands and children, to
be self-controlled and pure, to be busy at home, to be
kind, and to be subject to their husbands, so that no one
will malign the word of God" (Titus 2:3-5).

I first noticed her friendly manner at the checkout
counter of my grocery store. She always had a positive com-
ment to share with her customers, including me. She chided
when I didn't buy as much fruit as usual, and celebrated
with me when my coupons made a big difference in my grocery bill. Her manner was always teasing and upbeat. Senior
adults shopping there tried to get in her line. She was always
a ray of sunshine, even on a drab day. But one day, her face
was black and blue around her eyes.

"How did you get that shiner?" I asked as curiosity over-
came my manners.

"You don't want to know," was her solemn reply as she
cast her eyes downward. She finished ringing up my grocery
order in silence.

My rude curiosity quickly turned to compassion, and I
prayed for wisdom in reaching out to her.

"My name and phone number are on this paper. Call me

if I can help you," I said as I pressed a tract into her hand. I left the store praying in my heart for this hurting woman.

Three days later, my phone rang and a timid voice said, "Is this Betty Jo?"

"Yes."

"Well, you may not remember me, but I work at the grocery store."

"Pam!" I interrupted. And quickly assured her I did remember. "How can I help you?"

"Can you meet me today at 5:30 after I get off work?"

I did, and thus a pilgrimage began that reaped a new friend for me and briefly, a new lease on life for Pam. Her immediate need was for shelter. She was homeless because she had been living with an abusive boyfriend. She had a car, but it was not in running condition. The shelters for battered women were located too far from her job. Our county had no public transportation. Failing to find suitable housing, we invited Pam to live at our house for several months. Getting her car in running condition became a family project. It was like having a teenager again as we guided her along the path of driver's license tests, car tags and insurance, and piecing a jalopy together.

But thirty-four-year-old Pam's adult life was a life of abuse. Abused by a boyfriend, by strangers, by family, she in turn, abused herself. Pam abused alcohol. After a while we were heartsick to discover her chemical bondage. She was quite adept at hiding her addiction and her repressed anger and grief.

At times during those months, I wanted to cry the words of Jesus, "Stop sinning or something worse may happen to you" (John 5:14). At other times, Pam and I wept together as we prayed and acknowledged the love of our wonderful Savior and Lord.

Complete release still alludes Pam and waits on her to fully admit responsibility and ask for help. Support, encouragement, and resources are available through Christian friends, including her estranged family. But we all refuse to enable her self-destruction.

Domestic Violence

Domestic violence is on the rise in our society, transcending socioeconomic levels. The alarming awareness that abuse can and does happen to women regardless of their education or social position has destroyed the stereotypical scenario. Most of us might imagine policemen breaking in the door of a ramshackled house, a man in a drunken rage proclaiming loudly the absurdity of it all, and a woman cowering and crying in the corner. Unfortunately, such a scene is as likely to happen behind ornate doors of elegant homes with manicured lawns in posh suburbs.

Experts reveal that professional women who are victims of abuse are as prone, if not more apt, to deny and accept of responsibility for the abuse as are poorer, dependent women. In fact, some think that professional women who are extremely successful in their careers often fall prey to abuse by a less successful husband.

All abused women desperately want the abuse to be a passing, onetime event. Many times women refuse to acknowledge their victimization until their children also become victims.

Researchers have identified the pattern of abuse which they have named the "cycle of violence."[5] In the first stage, tension builds. The batterer, having temper tantrums which often result in damage to inanimate household objects, refuses to be reasonable. The couple needs to separate at this point.

The second stage is the battering, which may include slapping, hitting, kicking, or burning the victim, or sexual abuse. The battering can continue for hours or only a few minutes.

The third stage is the "honeymoon." In an effort to continue to exert power and control, the batterer becomes loving and apologetic. He may lavish the victim with gifts and promise the abuse will never happen again, especially if she doesn't provoke it. This cycle will happen again and again. There must be intervention.

Myths about battered women abound: they deserve the treatment; they are uneducated and have few job skills; and they are crazy. Myths about batterers include these: they have psychopathic personalities; they are never loving and attentive partners; they are violent in all their relationships; they are unsuccessful and lack resources to cope with the world; and once a batterer, always a batterer. Other myths include the idea that religious beliefs will prevent battering, and children need their father even if he is violent.[6]

Naively, people think the solution is simply to pack up and leave the abuser. But the road of escape is usually blocked with complex and confusing barriers that include fear of exposure and loss of reputation; fear of homicidal or suicidal tendencies of the husband; unequal access to financial funds; sporadic and diverse law enforcement by states.[7]

Tragically, the social ill of abuse also extends to the Christian community. During a conference for spouses of church staff members, a workshop on family violence was taught by an attorney. When she conducted an anonymous survey of the women present, she discovered a shocking fact: 75 percent of the attendees had experienced physical abuse. The time of the abuse was equally as shocking— mostly on Wednesday nights after a difficult business meeting at church.

These are some of the characteristics of an abuser. He . . .
- always has to be in charge of all decision-making in the home;
- feels he has little control of his life outside his house;
- sees his wife as property;
- treats the partner like a child, forcing her to ask permission to do things;
- exhibits low tolerance for stress;
- tends to have a Jekyll-and-Hyde personality;
- confuses love and violence;
- thinks it is OK to hit those he loves, usually as result of being abused himself;
- knows what he does and when he does it, but has poor recall due to denial;
- minimizes the violence or blocks it out completely;
- sees the victim as deserving the abuse;

- blocks out reality of himself as the cause of the violence;
- remains emotionally dependent;
- is always jealous and possessive;
- feels insecure and not worth loving or being loved;
- sees himself as absolute head of the household;
- views himself with low self-esteem;
- feels insecure about his sexuality;
- displays a rigid image of what a man ought to be;
- has overly traditional values.[8]

(Note: not every man who exhibits many of these character traits is necessarily an abuser.)

Recovery and Support Groups

Christian women are familiar and comfortable with women teaching women the Scripture, performing duties in the church, and fulfilling homemaking skills. But more unfamiliar territory to many of us includes ministering through support and recovery groups that help meet the crushing needs of women today.

One such recovery ministry is called HOPE (Healing of Past Abortion Experiences) in Kansas City, Missouri.[9] Mary Hurd, the founder, surveyed clinics throughout the metropolitan area and discovered only one abortion recovery ministry.

The survey uncovered calloused attitudes among social service agencies like, "We don't view abortion as a problem that anyone should grieve over in the first place. If there are women out there who are suffering emotionally because of their abortions, it's the fault of you Christians for placing such a load of guilt on them!"[10]

From her own experience, Mary Hurd knew better. She had been down the rocky road of rebellion and premarital sex, which left her with painful anxiety and grief. Drawing on the support and encouragement of forgiving parents, Mary began putting her life together by enrolling in a Christian college. There, she was received and discipled by Pastor Ray Leininger and his wife Judy. Graduating with a

degree in psychology with an emphasis in teen pregnancy
intervention and abortion counseling, Mary found employment in Kansas City at The LIGHT House, a crisis pregnancy center.

Her job and past experience became a catalyst for Mary
to start an abortion recovery group. She consulted her pastor about her perceived needs of women in the area. Pastor
Dale McConnell offered the use of First Calvary Church as a
meeting place for an abortion recovery group if Mary would
lead the group.

Mary's design for the group included a compassionate,
accepting, nonjudgmental atmosphere. The basic premise,
however, was that abortion and premarital sex are wrong.

"They'll never seek forgiveness if they don't see that
what they did was wrong. And they'll never get rid of their
pain unless they seek God's forgiveness," counsels Mary.[11]
She is extending her hand to women who have chosen
abortion. Meeting on Thursday evenings and studying a
course titled Women in Ramah, these women are being
healed and restored to abundant life.

Mary Hurd believes that angry shouts and accusations of
"murderer" may send more women into the abortion clinics.
Instead, she suggests volunteering in a crisis pregnancy center, sponsoring baby showers for unwed mothers, providing
meeting space within the church for support groups, developing a supportive, nonjudgmental relationship with an
pregnant teen or a woman who has elected to have an abortion, and praying that God will turn abortionists' hearts toward Him.

Sylvia Boothe, the Home Mission Board's coordinator
of Alternatives to Abortion Ministries, urges compassion
for women who are considering abortion or have already
experienced one. She continually emphasizes the ministry
aspect rather than becoming embroiled in the politics of
abortion. Women who have secretly aborted babies usually deny the grief they inevitably experience. Repressed
grief will deny women the forgiveness and closure they

desperately need. Some recovery groups encourage the giving of names to aborted infants and conducting memorial services so the mothers can experience closure to their grief.

Reach out and touch a friend who is weary;
Reach out and touch a seeker unaware;
Reach out and touch, though touching means losing
A part of your own self—If you dare!
Reach out and give your love to the loveless;
Reach out and make a home for the homeless;
Reach out and shed God's light in the darkness;
Reach out and let the smile of God touch thro' you.[12]

It is not God's will for any woman to be abused, imprisoned, or exploited. It is God's will for women to be healthy in body, soul, and spirit; and to be creative contributors to society and share in the redemption plan for all people. God does hold the whole world in His hands.

CHAPTER SIX

The Whole World in His Hands

He's got the whole world in His hands" are lyrics to a popular melody I remember singing since I was a little girl. My childish mind's eye always pictured literal and gigantic hands—God's hands—holding a colorful globe. But now, I know the song symbolically pictures the Creator lovingly holding the entire creation—an earth filled with people from all people groups—the whole world.

"For by him all things were created: things in heaven and on earth, visible and invisible, whether thrones or powers or rulers or authorities; all things were created by him and for him. He is before all things, and in him all things hold together" (Col. 1:16-17). "From one man he made every nation of men, that they should inhabit the whole earth; and he determined the times set for them and the exact places where they should live" (Acts 17:26).

The world that God holds in His hands is multicultural and multiracial home, but there is a common denominator for humanity. It is the lost condition of our souls due to sin and the dire need of a Savior to reconcile us to God. Culture and heritage are still celebrated by ethnic groups. Today, more and more, as diversity is appreciated, it is cause for celebration of all humankind. Our human need and our God-given purpose emphasizes our oneness.

As we search the Scriptures for God's view of the world, bigotry is replaced by full acceptance of each other as creatures of equal worth, dwelling in an earthly home created by God who loves each one and has a lovely plan for each human life. There is absolutely no place for feelings of supremacy, bigotry, or prejudice in the heart of a Christian reconciled to God. Such a person knows that salvation through the grace and mercy of God is bestowed upon and made available to everyone. Having a heart for missions is a good beginning to understanding and appreciating all of God's children.

The Origin of People Groups

Since the confusion of language at the Tower of Babel, recorded in Genesis 11, the world has been multilingual. Cultural diversity naturally followed linguistic diversity. The sin that entered the world through the disobedience of Adam and Eve is still reaping problems for all peoples. Adam and Eve became very much aware of the distinction between good and evil after they ate fruit from the tree of knowledge. In their shame and loss of innocence, they were banished from the Garden of Eden. Cherubim and a flamed sword guarded the gates to prevent entrance to the garden. If the primeval couple had indeed eaten from the tree of life, they would have lived forever, locked in their sinfulness, separated from God (Gen. 3:21-24).

Certainly, God's original plan included eternal life for Adam and Eve and all their offspring. But to mend their broken relationship with God and be redeemed, the couple needed much more than a piece of fruit.

Omnipotent, loving God set in motion the plan of salvation requiring a blood sacrifice. The heavenly Father promised to send a Savior. Jesus would fulfill the promise of salvation with His substitutionary and vicarious death on the cross for our sins. Jesus would meet the requirements of a holy God for the salvation of His creation.

From sinful Adam and Eve came sinful, wicked, and rebellious people. Noah and his family were the only righteous ones, so God destroyed the whole world's population, except for Noah's family, with a great flood.

Circumstances in the world didn't improve. The population increased in number. The people of the earth were ambitious, self-serving, and determined to be equal with God. Still speaking the same language, they planned to build a great city and a tower that they envisioned would reach the heavens (Gen. 11).

Once again, God intervened to thwart their selfish ambitions and steer them toward a God-serving attitude and lifestyle. Upon direct action from God, their language split into dialects indistinguishable to each other. Confusion reigned. Then the people scattered to different parts of the earth in groups according to their new speech patterns.

Beware! The scattering and confusion of the people from the Tower of Babel is not an indication of God's preference for one people group over another. Nor does sovereign God's selection of the people of Israel to be carriers of His redemption signal an exclusive God who plays favorites and redeems only those who meet His fancy. "The Lord is not slow in keeping his promise, as some understand slowness. He is patient with you, not wanting anyone to perish, but everyone to come to repentance" (2 Peter 3:9).

Simon Peter's Multiethnic Lesson

The Apostle Peter learned the inclusiveness of God's nature while in Caesarea at Cornelius' house. Peter was steeped in his cultural and religious upbringing that forbade association with Gentiles (all people who were not Jews).

Now, Peter had been with Jesus and had witnessed first-hand as Jesus transcended the social rules. Jesus had not been bound by culture and custom when He ministered to the Samaritan woman at the well in John 4. In answering the who-is-my-neighbor question, Jesus stung the Jewish inquirers by setting up a Samaritan man as a model of neighborly compassion (Luke 10:29-37).

Still Peter failed to catch the inclusiveness of the gospel. And, in his mind, if Gentiles could be saved, they would first have to embrace the Jewish religion and culture. But at Cornelius' house, thickheaded Peter seemed to finally understand. While on the roof, he saw the vision of the various animals, some clean and some unclean by Jewish dietary standards. Peter was instructed not to call any of them unclean—a contradiction of the Jewish system. In fact he was told he could eat any or all of the animals (Acts 10).

A confused and bewildered Peter became a strong and obedient Peter the next day as he spoke to the Gentiles in Cornelius' house. The vision of the ceremonially unclean animals was an object lesson from God to teach Peter the inclusiveness of the gospel for all people. No person is to consider another person racially unclean or impure. "You are well aware that it is against our law for a Jew to associate with a Gentile or visit him. But God has shown me that I should not call any man impure or unclean . . . I now realize how true it is that God does not show favoritism but accepts men from every nation who fear him and do what is right" (Acts 10:28, 34-35).

The Color of God's Hands

If God's hands were a color, they would surely be red, yellow, black, and white. Just like the children's song "Jesus Loves the Little Children," we are assured of God's love for all peoples, regardless of the color of their skin.

"For God so loved the world that he gave his one and only Son, that whoever believes in him shall not perish but have eternal life" (John 3:16). "He is the atoning sacrifice for our sins, and not only for ours [Jewish believers] but also for the sins of the whole world" (1 John 2:2).

It is not God's plan to save people through fruit which is eaten or not eaten, cities and towers built or not built, floods or natural disasters that befall the just and the unjust, but through His son Jesus. "This is how God showed his love among us: He sent his one and only Son into the world that we might live through him. This is love: not that we loved God, but that he loved us and sent his Son as an atoning sacrifice for our sins" (1 John 4:9-10). And so, the colorful, creative hands of God encompass a whole world of people groups with diverse cultures.

The Great Integration

"After this I looked and there before me was a great multitude that no one could count, from every nation, tribe, people and language, standing before the throne and in front of the Lamb. They were wearing white robes and were holding palm branches in their hands. And they cried out in a loud voice: 'Salvation belongs to our God, who sits on the throne, and to the Lamb.' All the angels were standing around the throne and around the elders and the four living creatures. They fell down on their faces before the throne and worshiped God, saying: 'Amen! Praise and glory and wisdom and thanks and honor and power and strength be to our God for ever and ever. Amen!' Then one of the elders asked me, 'These in white robes—who are they, and where did they come from?' I answered, 'Sir, you know.' And he said, 'These are they who have come out of the great tribulation; they have washed their robes and made them white in the blood of the Lamb. Therefore, 'they are before the throne of God and serve him day and night in his temple; and he who sits on the throne will spread his tent over them. Never again will they hunger; never again will they thirst. The sun will not beat upon them, nor any scorching heat. For the Lamb at the center of the throne will be their shepherd; he will lead them to springs of living water. And God will wipe away every tear from their eyes' " (Rev. 7:9-17).

This great doxology is sung by people from every nation. The graphic description of the Lamb's throne is one of complete integration of all races. From every nation, tribe, and language, they are standing before the throne of the Lamb of God, praising Him for their salvation and for bringing them through persecution and tribulation.

Persecution and tribulation are no respecters of people or race. Hunger, thirst, and scorching heat do not play favorites. Seemingly, no people group can justly claim exclusive prejudicial treatment. There is no denying the horrendous Holocaust of the Jewish people, the inhuman shipment of Africans for the slave trade, or the takeover of the Native American Indians' homeland. People of different races and cultures have clashed throughout history, but the crowd at the throne of Jesus includes every race praising God in the presence of Jesus.

Racial bigotry has no place in the lifestyle of a Christian. It is very unbecoming a child of God to profess love for God on the one hand and contempt for a brother on the other hand (1 John 2:9-11). There is reconciliation to be done—to God and to each other—and we must be about it. There is no time today to be racist or to practice racism with our lifestyle, while denying it with our mouths. Bigotry is a waste of precious energy and time.

Gerald Durley, African American pastor of Providence Baptist Church in Atlanta, Georgia, said, "We are past integration, today. We are talking reconciliation." A predominantly anglo congregation in the suburbs of Atlanta has joined hands with Rev. Durley by providing resources of people and finances to help rescue his community.

The promise is sure for our future: every nation, tribe, and language will be relieved from physical and spiritual perils suffered during their earthly pilgrimages. The Lamb of God, at His rightful place in the center, will shepherd all these peoples. They will be led to the thirst-quenching springs of living water. And the tears of the saved of every nation, tribe, and language will be wiped away. At last, wrongs will be righted, asymmetry will become symmetrical, imbalance, balanced. God's perfect will is done; redemption is complete.

The Great Segregation

God, at the Tower of Babel, brought segregation to the world so that He could gain man's attention. Man's sinfulness exaggerated and spawned an intensive segregation which pitted nation against nation. But, the greatest segregation, under God's authority, is yet to come. And it won't be based on language, culture, socioeconomic status, or color, but rather on each individual's response to Christ's offer of salvation and the resulting ministering lifestyle.

The Scripture warns of the great segregation completed by none other than the Lord Himself. " 'When the Son of Man comes in his glory, and all the angels with him, he will sit on his throne in heavenly glory. All the nations will be gathered before him, and he will separate the people one from another as a shepherd separates the sheep from the goats' " (Matt. 25:31-32). All the nations [people groups, not political entities] will be gathered before the Lord Jesus for judgment. The judgment is inclusive. No people groups are excluded. All will be called into accountability before the Lord God. All are in need of a Savior.

God's Rainbow Coalition

" 'All authority in heaven and on earth has been given to me. Therefore go and make disciples of *all nations* [author's emphasis], baptizing them in the name of the Father and of the Son and of the Holy Spirit, and teaching them to obey everything I have commanded you. And surely I am with you always, to the very end of the age' " (Matt. 28:18-20). From the book of beginnings (Genesis) to the book of endings (Revelation), even a casual reading of the Scriptures informs the reader of the original Creator of any rainbow coalition—God, Himself.

"Christianity is a white man's religion" scream some critics. Armed with their warped motto, leaders of godless cults and sects around the world are permeating unsuspecting people groups—people for whom Christ died and to whom salvation is freely offered. Missionaries who syncretize the gospel into various cultures without compromising scriptural principles are combating this criticism. They are reaping effective spiritual growth of new believers of every tribe and nation. Historically, some missionaries have made the mistake of converting (or attempting to convert) people to their culture as well as to the Christian faith. Most missionaries know this is ineffective, and it denies the competency of redeemed people to worship God.

Christianity invites all peoples to have a relationship with the Savior, the Son of God, and the invitation transcends all cultural or ethnic barriers. True, some are playing "catch up" in developing an acceptance of all nations, tongues, and people. In my opinion, a distinguishing mark of a Christian is openness to and full acceptance of all people, regardless of ethnic background. Imposing preferred worship styles on culturally diverse people limits the creativity of God Who made us all and receives worship directed toward Himself no matter the cultural context. The only requirement is that we worship Him "in spirit and in truth."

" 'The true worshippers will worship the Father in spirit and truth, for they are the kind of worshippers the Father seeks. God is spirit, and his worshippers must worship in spirit and in truth' " (John 4:23b-24).

One Woman Who Made a Difference

The Native American baby was pitiful. His face was distorted, and many thought he was brain-damaged. His parents were disappointed and had few hopes for this baby with so many problems.

The North Dakota Indian reservation either lacked medical facilities or the baby's plight was considered hopeless. So the baby grew into childhood suffering rejection from his family and humiliation from the community. His medical condition was actually a cleft palate, but his brain was completely normal. There was little solace, however, with the negative messages he received from all the people around him. His life was one of despair and loneliness. So much so, that as a child he spent his days at the dump playing with the rats. There, at least he could find food and warm clothing, as well as a strange camaraderie with the rats. The person who made a difference in Don Bartlett's life was a wealthy white woman. She employed Don's grandmother as a servant and noticed Don's condition. One day, according to his testimony, she sent for him. She had a job she thought he could do—wash her car. But he had never seen a car and had no idea how to wash one.

The woman patiently took a cloth and placed it in Don's hand. Gently placing her hand over his, she guided his hand in the motions of car washing. At the same time, she looked him in the eye and said softly, "I believe you can learn to do this." He describes the moment as magical. Never had he known such a gentle touch and never before had anyone offered him any confidence.

Today Dr. Don Bartlett is a Native American educator who contributes much to all cultures as well as to his own people. Once a lonely little boy who had a dump for his playground, Don discovered God's plan for his life because of the touch and affirmation of one Christian woman—a woman who planted the gospel seeds that later blossomed into a relationship with Christ.

The race and gender in the preceding true story are not important or relevant. Redeemed people of all colors and cultural backgrounds are making a difference as they allow God to work through them. The day of forced integration or segregation is gone. Today is a great day for reaching out and working together to carry the gospel of hope to all communities.

Southern Baptist Ethnic Leaders

When asked for their unique contributions to the cultural mix of Southern Baptist life, African American and ethnic Southern Baptists leaders responded with stories of hope and healing.

David Lee, of South Carolina, pointed out that most Chinese come from Buddhist backgrounds and a commitment to Christ is a serious commitment. "We do not take professions of faith [in Christ] lightly," he said. "We also bring into church life our reverence for hierarchy and our reverence for people who are older. We have a lot of respect in that way, and it takes effect in our churches."

"I think Hispanics bring a lot of passion, a lot of emotional commitment," remarked Oscar Medina of New York. "We tend to be a very emotional people, and as we accept Christ and come to Jesus, we make a whole life commitment. And we have a strong emotional attachment to our church."

"I think that ethnic youth can bring to the church the best of two cultures—their culture and the western culture. Our culture brings traditional values such as family loyalty, community involvement, and respect," said Seilavong Doeung, Cambodian leader from Dallas, Texas. "But we also incorporate the western ideals of individualism, determination, and freedom. It creates a powerful tool and opportunity for ministry. Youth are also in a position to promote a better understanding between the Anglo and ethnic churches. The Cooperative Program has been very effective and helpful, and I hope it will continue as these young people become older and take their places in the churches."

The Russian leader, Sergei Nikolaev, reminded us, "Anglo culture is very individualistic, Slavic is very collective. Theologically, western culture concentrates on what God has done for us through Jesus Christ, period. Russian culture takes the next step—what can we do as a response to what the Lord has done. I think it's pure living, the tendency to please God, not to pay for salvation, but to keep the high standard of the spiritual life. American Christians very often speak about the acceptance of Christ into their heart which makes a person a Christian. Russians always speak about the conversion, the 180-degree turn, the completely new life with God. One thing I meet with in Western culture is a lot of doubt about the Bible. For Slavic culture every word of the Bible is the divine revelation from the Lord. A lot of Russian Christians are coming to the United States, and they bring a strong heritage of Christianity. But there are many things that Russians can learn from Anglos, as well as we can also contribute a new dimension and blessing into Anglo churches."

Victor Kaneubbe, a Native American leader from Arizona said, "I want to mention three things: (1) There is no time limit to the service; we just go until we get through; (2) There's not much formality; it's a free service. We may schedule a worship service, but we are willing to be interrupted by things that just happen to come, things we thought we ought to express rather than just pass by. For example, a drunk may come forward, and I will call some or all alcoholic Christians to come forward and pray for that person. We'll let the missions organizations have some special part on Sunday Morning (WMU installation; Lottie Moon play) when we have our largest crowd, so they'll be informed about what our church is doing; (3) Many of our churches sing hymns, preach and have their service in their own tribal language."

And Michael Thurman, African American leader from Georgia, offered, "I would say these are the contributions of African American culture to SBC life: (1) powerful and potent spirituality; (2) a holistic approach to ministry; (3) a dynamic worship style; (4) new models of church growth and governance.[1]

Suburbs and Inner City

Geographical barriers are falling. The suburban-dwelling
Christians, whatever their color, can no longer afford to
cast their pity toward the inner cities while feeling smug
and secure. It's just a matter of time until the problems of
the inner city pierce the suburbs. In many places, it's already happening. God is working to bring resources of
people and gifts to the inner cities where scores of adults
and children need the sincere milk of the Word and the
cleansing acceptance of a Savior who loves them and
gave Himself for them.

I see the hands of Jesus working through Kathy
Tucker, a gifted single woman who lives where three
communities converge in inner-city Atlanta, Georgia.
The people who make up the communities are Anglo,
African American, and Hispanic. In 1987, Kathy moved
into a former antique store in Cabbagetown, the low-in-
come Anglo neighborhood. Recently recommitted to the
Lord, Kathy began reaching out to scores of neighborhood children by giving them cookies and soft drinks.
That simple act has turned into a thriving ministry of
love in action to hundreds of children and their families.
Her ministry emphasizes prayer and worship, but includes food distribution as well as limited medical services. Kathy networks with the secular Atlanta
community as well as the churches for resources to use
as she touches her neighbors for Jesus.

A ride through the streets with Kathy yields smiles,
waves, giggles, and hugs from the residents. She is an angel of mercy and ministry. Because of prayer, she feels
uninhibited in her ministry. Thursdays and Saturdays are
children's church days. They come to her house to sing
and to memorize and study Scripture. After corporate
sponsors showered hundreds of children with expensive
gifts at Christmas, Kathy noticed selfishness and material-
istic attitudes developed in some of the children. She
combated the harmful attitudes by teaching the ones who

had received new toys to give their used ones to others. The children Kathy first began working with are now teenagers. She is attempting to instill scriptural leadership qualities in them.

Laborers for her ministry come from without and within. Conrad, an African American and former crack cocaine addict, is an example to the community of the transforming power of Christ in his life. One day, Kathy saw Conrad on the street and stopped him. She put her arms around him and began praying for Jesus to deliver him from drugs. Eventually, he experienced salvation for his soul as well as deliverance from his chemical dependency. Today, he assists Kathy in the ministry and has found complete newness of life with fulfillment and purpose. Recently a mother with a drug addiction wanted to start over and get "what Conrad had." Plans are underway for her to join a Scripture-based recovery group.

A Mosaic in the Hands of God

With the flow of immigrants into the country, the United States has been called a melting pot. Such a metaphor implies immigrants coming from diverse countries and losing their heritage because they undergo a "melting" into the culture of the United States.

Actually, the United States is a mosaic. More than 500 ethnic groups—each with their own distinctiveness—are an artistic collage of culture and diversity. Nearly 120 million people identify with a ethnic group or speak a language other than English. These millions of people speak some 636 languages and dialects. "Already the Southern Baptist Convention is the most integrated denomination in American. Every Sunday Southern Baptists worship and study the Bible in 102 languages and dialects. More than 6,588 language-culture congregations/units—with about 500,000 members—are affiliated with Southern Baptist associations, state conventions, and the Southern Baptist Convention. God is moving among ethnic Americans."[2]

Some of the strongest churches in the Southern Baptist Convention are ethnic churches. The First Haitian Baptist Church in Boston is a French-speaking congregation with 800 in attendance. Pastor Verdieu Laroche serves on the executive board of the Baptist Convention of New England and was part of the search committee to call an executive director. Their ministry to children is a blessing in spite of few resources. As many as 40 children in a class sit on backless benches, elbow to elbow (with no room to wiggle). The little ones listen with fixed attention to one teacher. The church has Sunday School in every imaginable place in their cramped building. Any extra funds are sent to their homeland of Haiti to help the many needs there.

The largest church in the Baptist Convention of Maryland/Delaware is the Korean-speaking Global Mission Church in Silver Spring, Maryland. Dr. Man-Poong Dennis Kim is the senior pastor and co-pastors with Dr. Daniel Lee. Attendance is well over 1,100 and they have hosted the annual state convention meeting with royal hospitality. A well-rounded program of evangelism and Bible teaching for all ages is reaching several generations of Koreans.

A Southern Baptist African American church in Houston, Texas, is one of the largest congregations of any denominations in the United States. Brentwood Baptist Church, with Pastor Joe Ratliff who has served Houston's Union Baptist Association as moderator, has 11,000 members. The 1994 attendees of the Southern Baptist Convention in Houston were thrilled with the Brentwood Drill Team of more than 100 young people in uniform, performing Bible memory exercises in perfect cadence and rhythm. The church reaches its community and beyond with evangelistic apartment ministries and sponsorship of several new works.

A very active Southern Baptist Church and one of the top three or four in Cooperative Program giving is the

Tacoma First Baptist Church, Tacoma, Washington. The Korean-speaking congregation has four worship services on Sunday morning. Three are conducted in Korean; one is conducted in English for second-generation Koreans. The congregation, with approximately 850 in attendance, averages several baptisms weekly. Pastor Chang Sun Moon led the church to start a congregation in Bothell, a suburb of Seattle. The pastor of the new congregation first served the Tacoma First Baptist Church as an intern. A key to the effectiveness of this church is the daily prayer meetings at 5:30 A.M. The members come to the church to pray before going to work. Then, on Friday nights, the church gathers to pray into the wee hours of Saturday morning.

Andrea's Hands Are God's Hands in Oregon

God's hands were on a little girl, an "army brat," many years ago. He used her parents, even though they were not professing Christians, to instill in her a keen interest in the local culture, language, and people during the family's military assignments.

Andrea, as a part of God's plan, lived three years in Germany, learning its language and culture. As she grew up, she continued to develop her love for people of other cultures. Years later, while the family was stationed in Taiwan, Andrea received Jesus Christ into her life. Her salvation was the direct result of a friend's prayers. Their fathers had worked together in Washington, D.C., at the Pentagon. When the Christian friend heard that Andrea's family was assigned to Taiwan, she wrote her friends in the American school to "watch for Andrea."

Consequently, Andrea, the new teenager on the block, found a new social circle—friends who were Christians. Her new routine included an exciting Christian youth group led by missionaries and church twice on Sundays. All were strange to Andrea, but she soon embraced God's love in her heart and committed her life to Him.

Andrea remembers, "After I was saved, no one told me that God was supposed to impact my life and plans." But that is exactly what happened. Teenaged Andrea combined her love and appreciation for different cultures with her new faith in Christ, experiencing an early call into cross-cultural ministries.

After her marriage to Clint Ashley, the two of them went to Brazil as Southern Baptist missionaries to the Portuguese-speaking people. The fluent-in-German American, with Asian ties, found herself in Portuguese language school. After language school, the Ashleys served six years in Brazil. Leaving there in 1978, they ministered together in the Northwest and Canada. In 1992, the couple moved to Gresham, Oregon, where Clint directs the Northwest Campus of Golden Gate Seminary.

"I speak the wrong foreign language! I don't know a single Brazilian in Oregon," wailed Andrea. Looking for an outlet for cross-cultural ministry, Andrea couldn't figure out where to plug into service for the Lord. But she began noticing the great influx of Hispanics into the Northwest from Central and South America.

"Lord, do you want me to learn another language?" prayed Andrea. With assurance of direct leadership from God, she soon enrolled in Mt. Hood Community College to study Spanish.

Three weeks after the Spanish class began, Andrea questioned everything about her ministry commitment and future. She was told the cancer she had been free of for five-and-one-half years had recurred, and it proved to be inoperable. Facing uncertainty, she and husband joined together in prayer. As they prayed for leadership, they decided together that Andrea should cancel all speaking engagements at retreats and conferences. She would clear her calendar of outside activities except Spanish classes. This meant Andrea would go only to class and then to radiation and later, as treatment progressed, to chemotherapy. She studied Spanish for three to five hours a day. Medical people call this kind of activity "distraction therapy." Unwittingly, Andrea was helping her physical condition by living out her commitment to missions because one of the best "medicines" for cancer patients is to focus on something besides the disease.

Cancer free again, Andrea continues to immerse herself in the Spanish language. Every day she reads a modern language Spanish Bible, the *Dios Habla Hoy*. She enjoys the Spanish version of *Reader's Digest* and does her ironing and drives her car while listening to Spanish tapes—always asking God to give her the language so she can communicate His love to the many Hispanics in the Portland area.

The rippling effect of Andrea's hands in God's hands is the resulting network among Hispanics. Andrea excitedly calls it a phenomenal act of God. Neighbors on her street from Uruguay, Peruvian friends in the community, a group of Central American students at the community college, and people in a predominantly Hispanic apartment complex are learning of God's love as they are impacted by the gospel Andrea carries to them in their heart language.

Andrea ministers in the Iglesia Evangélica Vida Nueva in Gresham, Oregon. She conducts a weekly prayer group, a Bible study that focuses on one passage of Scripture (usually having to do with prayer) per meeting, and responds in a mentoring way to the issues in the women's lives. She has been a Bible teacher for women in the Vida Nueva congregation and the all-Northwest Hispanic family camp.

Andrea finds, after 35 years of ministry, that women's issues are cross-cultural. Many women need counseling and encouragement in their difficult marriages. Hispanic women in this country often feel isolated and desperate, and Andrea is there to be a sounding board as they apply scriptural principles to the situation.

"I've learned your language so I can tell you about God's love," is a usual opening as Andrea and her Spanish partners go door-to-door in the Hispanic apartment complex. Her motto and strength come from Hebrews 13:20*a*, 21. "May the God of peace . . . equip you with everything good for doing his will, and may he work in us what is pleasing to him, through Jesus Christ, to whom be glory for ever and ever. Amen."

Andrea's life is a testimony of her belief in the equipping power of God. In her case, God has given her a gift of language which, through His strength for her health and energy, she has developed.

All of us are so equipped, not with the same gift, but with a unique one, with the assumption that we will work hand in hand with each other.

CHAPTER SEVEN

Hand in Hand with Each Other

"No man is an island, entire of itself; every man is a piece of the continent, a part of the main . . ." Long before John Donne wrote this poem, the Apostle Paul declared the same truth in the letter to the Christians at Rome. "For none of us lives to himself alone and none of us dies to himself alone" (Rom. 14:7). Paul taught that since Christians belong to the Lord, they must also relate to one other. Relationship is an integral piece of our lives. It is who we are; it is how we work.

While most women thrive in ministries of hospitality, caregiving, and reaching out to others, the way God works in and through us is as diverse and individual as each person. The way He uses us this year may be distinctly different from next year. One thing remains constant: God's desire to work through His people.

Even though there is so much wrong in our society, it is much easier to pull inside ourselves and fight for our own existence and sanity. It's easy to rationalize: what can one person or family do to change the course of a nation?

Someone observed the work of Mother Teresa and determined it somewhat ineffective because of her focus on the needs of individuals. In light of the vast needs of her country, India, her charitable deeds might seem pitifully small and sluggish. When asked about her mundane work, she merely answered, "God has called me to help these people—one by one."

Government aid programs do help people here and there, but the daily news is replete with failures of bureaucracies. Relief seldom trickles down to the target group. And we are not excused from one-on-one ministry even though much aid and assistance is disbursed through our government.

Because the needs are overwhelming, we are lulled into apathy. The tax revenue of our nation, the tithes to our church, as well as the sacrificial gifts we designate, may soothe our consciences and convince us we are doing enough.

But compassionate people and ministering churches are capturing a vision of reaching out and touching people in their communities, especially those who do not attend any church. People ministering to people on a small scale may be more economically efficient than broadly based programs with huge overhead costs. Hand in hand indicates individual with individual as well as individuals with God. It calls for very personal involvement. We cannot hide in the church building or beneath the banner of our denomination. The tax revenue of this great nation cannot bear the burdensome cost of ministry that God's people are meant to do.

Women can lead the way in helping their churches catch a vision of being God's hands in ministry. There are enough human resources in the Christian community to obliterate much human suffering. Christians must come out of the safety of their church buildings and homes, pinpoint needs, then mix and integrate to fulfill needs.

Toby Frost, associate director of the Mass Evangelism department of the Home Mission Board, thinks what many of us do is akin to a team huddle in a football game. He sees Christians huddling in church buildings and retreating into Bible studies, worship services, each other's homes, or going in groups to local restaurants—oblivious to outsiders, but safe in the group. We are in danger of too much huddling. This proliferation of Christian subgroups—people who remain in tight-knit circles of Christians—threatens our commission to evangelize. The big difference in Christian huddles and the football team is that after a game huddle, the football players join the game. There is an end to the huddling.

One of Toby's biggest fears is that someone will build a subdivision and stores where only Christians may live and shop. Imagine, he said, "a grocery store where only Christians can buy groceries like glorified garden vegetables and sanctified soap flakes."

That may seem tempting, but wait. Heaven, "the sweet by and by," where only Christians live, comes after life on this earth. We live in the here and now, which someone called "the nasty now and now," and that is precisely where we are called to live and make a difference for Christ. Regardless of the type of community we live in, there is need. People may be up-and-out or down-and-out. People may be going to heaven when they die, but what about their messed-up lives now?

Needs may be across state and county lines or next door. Scales must be lifted from our eyes so we can see through the eyes of Jesus. We have pulled a cloak of isolation around our families. We even drive our cars while sitting behind darkly tinted windows. We make sure our children mix with the "right" group, equip our homes with security alarms, and look scornfully at those who are different in our churches or communities. And in the name of protecting something valuable to us, we have lost the excitement and blessing of ministry.

Jim Elliot, a martyred missionary to Ecuador in the '50s, wrote in his diary, "No man is a fool who gives what he cannot keep to gain what he can never lose."[1]

While we in the church are trying to decide if jeans are appropriate dress, if hair is the proper length, or

whether or not to wear an earring, our communities are
disintegrating around us. Such disintegration occurs not
as the result of what one wears, but over real problems
like homelessness, abusive husbands, untimely pregnan-
cies, illiteracy, substance abuse, violence, and neglected
children.

No longer can we cry, "That has nothing to do with
me. I am a law-abiding citizen, and I'm contributing my
goodness to society. I mind my own business. I don't get
in anyone's way." Are we really satisfied making such a
passive contribution to society? Such negative introver-
sion is very unbecoming to a redeemed person.
Aggressive ministry lifestyles that reach out and touch in
the name of Jesus are much more fulfilling. Selfish, in-
grown lifestyles are pitifully predictable and boring.
Accept a challenge! Our lives can be exciting and un-
predictable through ministry to others.

Corrie ten Boom, the watchmaker's daughter from
Holland, says her life was very ordinary with a predictable routine until she was past 50 years of age. Her
family lived together, worked together, and worshipped
together in prewar Holland. Then came World War II.
Her father's Christian convictions would not allow him
to idly observe the persecution of his Jewish neighbors
and friends. So they began hiding them from the gestapo
in the ten Boom home. The story of their subsequent im-
prisonment is written in her book, *The Hiding Place*.

"But, really, we'll take comforting boredom over in-
carceration in a German concentration camp," we cry.
"Look what ministering to oppressed people earned the
ten Boom family."

Then the thoughtful truth spoken by someone: God
only gives dying grace on dying days. It is impossible to
store up enough grace to be ready for every Satanic on-
slaught that comes our way. However, the marvelous
grace of God comes to us in timed-release capsules with
just the right amount of strength in ratio to our adversity.

God's hands are really the safest place to be, and His grace is sufficient. With our hands in God's hands, our lives can be a pilgrimage of ministry which shuts out all complacency. Sensitive women are natural leaders in organizing ministry. We must make an effort to reach out and make a difference in someone's life. Everyone is connected to others through relationships in families or at work—no one is an island, living completely to herself or himself. A ministry to one person often ripples out to that person's family and friends.

A where-do-you-hurt-and-how-can-I-help mentality of churches goes a long way in discovering people in pain and winning them into God's kingdom. The best way to win someone to Christ is by ministering to the individual's needs. Ministry earns an entrance into hearts and homes. The concept of "break-out" ministries urges Christians to come out of their church buildings, their families, their traditions, their paradigms to develop community ministries.

Approximately 50 percent of Southern Baptist churches are involved in ministry, but many such ministries are within the church family only. By the year 2000, we hope to see 75 percent of our churches ministering to the church family as well as reaching out to their communities. The hardest heart of an unredeemed person may be softened and made pliable when receiving ministry, or even when observing a Christian ministering to a hurting person.

One young minister recalls that his family was saved because a pastor helped his daddy chop wood. The pastor came to visit and witness. But daddy didn't have time to listen to the gospel presentation; he had to chop wood. The next time the pastor showed up, he was dressed in his wood-chopping clothes. Daddy and his whole household were saved. The young minister's own ministry was shaped by the example of the older pastor who, through God-given sensitivity, earned the right to share the gospel with the daddy.

My favorite description of Christianity declares it is not simply a religion but a relationship. Definitions of most religions depict people trying to reach God by acquiring knowledge, doing good deeds, embracing philosophies, or some self-effacing method. But Christianity uniquely portrays God as coming down to people in the person of Jesus Christ and seeking a relationship with them.

Thus, we relate to one another. We are to work hand in hand with God and with each other. There is no time to criticize, condemn, or destroy. There is work to be done, and we must each be part of it.

Remember when the disciples asked Jesus about someone's ministry and Jesus cautioned, "for whoever is not against you is for you" (Luke 9:50)?

I was taught to appreciate all types of music. Of course, I have my favorites that minister to me and enhance my worship. However, God receives all music offered to Him in worship. The only Biblical pattern for worship style is the Jewish model. And I don't see many Baptist churches with that style! God has a greater capacity of reception than you or me. Therefore, we should not be scrutinizing and setting one kind against another. The genius of God has allowed for uniqueness among individuals. Our uniqueness is bound to yield different styles of music and service. All of it is valid in the kingdom.

We Need Each Other

Working hand in hand with each other requires a recognition of different gifts as well as a knowledge of one's own spiritual gift or gifts. In 1 Corinthians 12, spiritual gifts are compared to different parts of the body, each a significant part of the whole. A body which consists of only one or a few parts is hardly an efficient body. Likewise, the church is much more efficient with members who, knowing their gifts, all work together. It will take all of us recognizing and developing our gifts to do the greater works which Jesus promised we would do.

There is a woman in your sphere of influence who needs you. She needs to know what you know, and you need to share what you have. She may need your friendship and encouragement.

There is a child where you live or work who will go hungry, be abused, or enter a life of violence if you don't use your gifts to reach out to that young life.

There is an ethnic person or group where you live or work who will never know Jesus if you don't teach them to read, shop, and live in this strange culture.

For His own reasons, God has chosen people to tell people about Him and the salvation He freely offers. With the acceptance of the good news of the gospel which saves from eternal separation from God, there is a promise of abundant life right now.

Knowing Jesus personally and submitting ourselves to His service is abundant living. To be the hands, the feet, the voice, or the compassion of Jesus is the exciting privilege of every Christian.

Hear His words once again: "I tell you the truth, anyone who has faith in me will do what I have been doing. He will do even greater things than these, because I am going to the Father" (John 14:12). The promise has only one condition—our positive response!

Notes

Chapter 2

[1]Thomas Curtis Clark, T*he Touch of Human Hands, in 1,000 Quotable Poems: An Anthology of Modern Verse,* comp. Thomas Curtis Clark and Esther A. Gillespie (New York: Harper and Brothers, 1937) pp. 37-38.

Chapter 4

[1]Edith Shaeffer, *What Is a Family?* (Grand Rapids, MI: Baker Book House, 1975) 47.

[2]Mark Wingfield, "The Quality of Childhood is Deteriorating," *Word and Way,* 11 August 1994. First published by Associated Baptist Press.

[3]Tere Seeley, "People who can't read costing us all," *The Atlanta-Journal Constitution,* 29 May 1994.

[4]Gary Fields, "Disturbing similarity: Two sisters slain," *USA Today,* 25 November 1994.

[5]Gary Fields, "1.6 million kids home alone," USA Today, 20-22 May 1994.

[6]Statistics are the result of a random survey taken at the 1993 Southern Baptist Convention.

[7]Denise George, "Protecting Church Children From Sexual Abusers," *The Christian Index,* 23 June 1994.

[8]Bill Moyers, *Violence: A PBS Special,* 9 January 1995.

[9]Poem by Sergeant Jim E. Williams, Oklahoma City Police Department. First published in the *International Police Chaplains Magazine.* Reprinted with permission.

Chapter 5

[1]From *Let Me Be a Woman* by Elisabeth Elliot. © 1976 by Tyndale House Publishers, Inc. Used by permission. All rights reserved.

[2]Parenthetical statements belong to Ron Dunn, evangelist and Bible teacher, Texas.

[3]*Women 1994: Indicators of Opportunity for Christian Witness and Ministry,* fourth annual edition (McLean, VA: Women's Department of the Baptist World Alliance) 1994.

[4]Proclamation of Good News for Women, (McLean, VA: Women's Department of the Baptist World Alliance) 1992.

[5]Information from the Council on Battered Women, P. O. Box 54383, Atlanta, GA 30308.

[6]Ibid.

[7]Hillary Johnson, "The Truth about White-collar Domestic Violence," *Working Women,* March 1995, 55.

[8]River View Counseling Center, Waco, Texas.

[9]Brenda Sanders, "Healing Abortion's Aftermath," *Word and Way,* 1 September, 1994.

[10]Ibid.

[11]Ibid.

[12]"Reach Out" (*Baptist Hymnal,* 1975 edition). Words and tune REACH OUT, Charles F. Brown, 1971. © Copyright 1971 by Word, Inc. Arr. © 1975 by Word Music, Inc. All rights reserved. Used by permission.

Chapter 6

[1]Reprinted from "What does your ethnic group bring to the SBC?", SBC Life, May 1994. Used with permission.

[2]"Heirs of Faith" (Atlanta, GA: Home Mission Board, 1992).

Chapter 7

[1]Elisabeth Elliot, *Shadow of the Almighty* (San Francisco: Harper & Row Publishers, 1958) 247.

Teaching Plan

These plans are for a 2½-hour study; adapt as necessary. Encourage participants to read the book prior to the study.

Preparation

- Make posters of the book and chapter titles.
- Draw seven hands on sheets of paper; write these words or names: Hands in Scripture; God's Hands; Jesus' Hands; Moses' Hands; Paul's Hands; Eager Hands; Ministering Hands.

Introduction (10 minutes)

Ask participants to think about their hands (use suggestions on pp. 7-8). Ask them to think of things that cannot be done with one hand, or that can be best done with two or more hands.

First Session (1 hour)

- Arrange participants into four groups; ask each group to review and report on one of the four sections of Chapter 1.
- Distribute the seven sheets of paper with hands drawn on them. Ask participants to find this section of Chapter 2, prepare a brief review, and suggest lessons this example has for them. Two or three participants may work together.
- Discuss the potter, the clay, and how these illustrate our relationship to God (Chapter 3). Ask, What are the blessings of being clay in the potter's hands? Ask participants to recall times in their lives they have felt this kind of relationship to God.
- Ask participants to list problems today's children face. Write responses on a chalkboard. Review the facts on page 33.

Make another list of ways Jesus demonstrated His attitude about children. Ask, In light of Jesus' teachings, what can we do about the plight of the children in our nation? In addition to general answers, encourage participants to think of specific actions they can take.

Break

Second Session (1 hour)

- Ask participants to write a paragraph describing the importance of women in the kingdom of God (Chapter 5). After a few participants share what they wrote ask, Why do women need to realize this truth? What happens when they do not realize they are important in the kingdom? Review the facts on pages 51-52. Allow participants to recall experiences they have had when they had the challenge of ministering to or working with someone experiencing one or more of these circumstances. Use the Proclamation (pp. 53-54) as a responsive reading. Write the words mentoring, support groups, and advocacy on a large sheet of paper. Ask participants to discuss ways these activities can minister to hurting women. Again, encourage participants to think of and make commitments to specific actions they can take.
- Review Simon Peter's experience (pp. 63-64 and Acts 10). Ask, If we as a nation (church, community, etc.) truly believed that God loves all people equally, what difference would it make? What specific steps can we take to begin to make this difference?

Conclusion (20 minutes)

Review the chapter title posters. Ask participants to share something they learned during the study (a new idea for ministry, a fact they did not know, a new insight or understanding of God and His plan for their lives, etc.). Encourage participants to make one specific commitment to a change they will make, ministry they will begin, or other action. Close in prayer.